COLOR & TEXTURE
For the Rigid Heddle Loom

A Study in Yarn Selection for Weavers

Tamara Poff

Poff Studio

Copyright © 2018 Tamara Poff

All rights reserved.

ISBN: 978-0-9984590-1-1

1

Poff Studio

Tucson, Arizona 85737

www.poffstudio.com

Layout and Design: Tamara Poff

Photography and Art Direction: Jill Greenop

Editor: Mikaela Koncija

Technical Editor: Lynn Lee

Handspun Yarn used in pattern on p. 46 created by Mikaela Koncija

Yarn weight symbols, standard body measurements, and project levels source: Craft Yarn Council's www.YarnStandards.com

©2018 Tamara Poff

All rights reserved. No part of these pages, either text or image, may be used for any purpose other than personal use. Therefore, reproduction, modification, storage in a retrieval system, or retransmission in any form or by any means, electronic, mechanical, or otherwise, for reasons other than personal use, is strictly prohibited without prior written permission from the publisher.

It is to you, my rigid heddle weavers, seeking the bold and venturous path into ever more creative frontiers with just simple tools, that I dedicate this effort.

Contents

34

39

45

46

54

58

64

68

78

86

90

98

104

110

Acknowledgements

I am blessed to be surrounded by many talented and wonderful people who have contributed to this work. First, my beautiful models: step daughters-in-law, Kristie and Karolynn Poff, and daughter, Ashley Milhizer.

Also, I am graced with sister, Jill Greenop, whose amazing skill with people and the camera make producing this book a true pleasure.

Lastly, many thanks to my supportive and loving husband who makes it all possible, giving up many months of our time together to see these pages to fruition.

Love you all.

A special thanks to my friends at the recently retired, Mango Moon Yarn Company of Owosso, Michigan for lending us their space, Sue, Laurie, and Lisa...and an extra thanks to Sue for opening up for us after hours!

Hangin' Out in Yarn Shops…

I learned how to knit before my 5th birthday. Delivering me as the 2nd of four children, my mother needed a distraction for me and my older sister, once number 3 and 4 (twins) arrived; thus, we became the gleeful makers of some very raggedly Barbie doll coats back then. From here, my love of fiber was born. I realized early on that I was never more profoundly at home than when I was surrounded by lots of yarn. I became a frequenter of yarn shops, spinning groups, and weaving shops where I could find them. I even owned a yarn shop for a while with number 4 until we decided it was more likely my dream, her nightmare.

If you share my addiction, and you've taken up the little loom craft, do ever find yourself trying to explain what drives you to rigid heddle weaving? I maintain that it is largely that awesome surprise that comes with each new weaving venture, no matter what your level of experience (and the gratification that comes with getting to that surprise so quickly).

The rigid heddle loom is a tool that was born for beautiful yarn. Because it puts less stress on the ends than our larger cousin (the multi-harness, floor loom), our loom is a star at showcasing the best in color, novelty textures, and exotic fibers that we covet in our local yarn shops. With all the choices therein, the number one question I am asked in my years of teaching is, "What can I weave with?" (p. 25). There is an understandable fear that one could find oneself in the middle of a large investment of time and money only to arrive at the epic fail of unstable, or at the other end, stiff-as-a-board fabric, and/or unsightly color combinations. Sometimes the later frustration is voiced as, "I just don't have a sense for color!" (p. 17).

The 2nd most common roadblock to expanding rigid heddle horizons is the fear of altering our woven rectangles with the cutting, stitching, embellishing we employ to make a wearable garment. What if we screw things up?

If you recognize yourself here, fear not, wielders of the craft! In this 2nd book of the series to help rigid heddle weavers "go beyond the rectangle", I will expand on my discoveries as a painter and a yarn handler to lend you a structure to proceed more confidently and to keep the "awesome" in the surprise.

At right: colorful display at Mobile Yarn, Mobile, Alabama

Let's Begin...
How to Use this Book

My wish for you,

is that you will approach the making of fabric on your rigid heddle loom with a confidence to produce ever more beautiful and diverse weaving. Garment creation can be intimidating in the beginning. Offering this 2nd book in my series of teaching patterns, I hope to help you avoid some of the pitfalls of our craft and assist you in putting together the colors, textures, and yarn weights that lead to more wearable pieces.

Yarn Substitution

The garments created for this book spring from the quality yarns found primarily in a knitter's world. This is where we locate the most tempting and exciting fibers to invest in for our handwork. Also, the gauge of the yarns used for knitting is the ideal range for rigid heddle looms.

As is true of the business, yarns enter and exit as seasons change, and providers come and go. For this reason, and because you may choose to substitute, I provide the actual yardage, the gauge of each yarn used, and yarn advice at the beginning of each pattern. This will help if you make alternate choices.

Warp Test

If you do alter the yarns used, don't forget to test whether your yarn choice is strong enough to be warp. To do this, hold the yarn in one hand, then grab the strand in your other hand with about 12" in between. Pull forward against this length to simulate the amount of pressure your loom might put on the yarn. You want to be sure it doesn't break easily under moderate pressure.

Since you can seldom test the warp yarn before you buy it, the pattern on p. 34 gives you an idea for what you can do if your warp choice fails once you get it home.

About Gauge

I will refer to the Standard Yarn Weight System of the Craft Yarn Council of America (www.craftyarncouncil.com) to describe most of the yarns used in these patterns. A clip from their online chart is included for reference on p. 29. You don't have to be a knitter or crocheter to understand and use this system. Most knitting yarns will have the yarn number and/or the stitches per 4" swatch, along with the needle sizes recommended, on the label for you, so take this book with you to cross reference when you are shopping.

Getting the right yarn gauge to reed size and understanding how that translates into the fabric you desire, is a big part of your journey to success and is discussed extensively throughout the book.

Navigating the Patterns

Each pattern begins with general observations about the garment and the **degree of difficulty** for that piece. I've borrowed from and modified a system established by the Craft Yarn Council to attempt to assess the level of expertise required for weaving and the degree of sewing skills needed (where applicable). See my definition of Degree of Difficulty on p. 12.

A few of the patterns are embellished with a minimal amount of simple knitting and/or crochet to enhance shape, fit, and drape. However, when possible, I've included a weaving work-around for those who don't knit or crochet.

Instead of naming the patterns, I've labeled them by **the challenge** represented in that work and will detail that challenge in the green box each time.

You'll find dimensions for **choosing size** next. Additional measurements, if applicable, may be given in diagrams with page references here which will be useful for desired alterations. Size changes are given in parenthesis in the patterns. I recommend that you become familiar with the amount of ease (clearance in width that fits you best) and

the lengths that suit you, so you can alter accordingly.

When I specify minimum loom widths in the equipment section, I break them down in increments offered by 6 major loom manufacturers so you can see if you have enough loom width for that pattern at a glance.

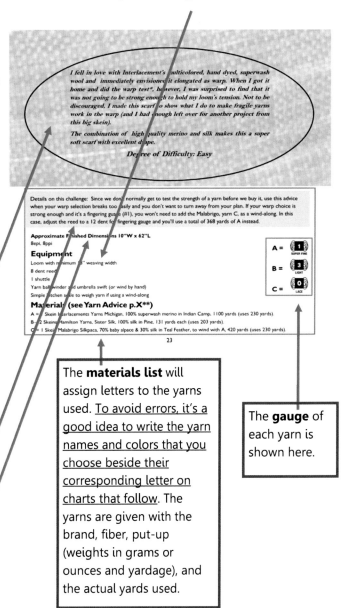

I fell in love with Interlacement's multicolored, hand dyed, superwash wool and immediately envisioned it elongated as warp. When I got it home and did the warp test*, however, I was surprised to find that it was not going to be strong enough to hold my loom's tension. Not to be discouraged, I made this scarf to show what I do to make fragile yarns work in the warp (and I had enough left over for another project from this big skein).

The combination of high quality merino and silk makes this a super soft scarf with excellent drape.

Degree of Difficulty: Easy

Details on this challenge: Since we don't normally get to test the strength of a yarn before we buy it, use this advice when your warp selection breaks too easily and you don't want to turn away from your plan. If your warp choice is strong enough and it's a fingering gauge (#1), you won't need to add the Malabrigo, yarn C, as a wind-along. In this case, adjust the reed to a 12 dent for fingering gauge and you'll use a total of 368 yards of A instead.

Approximate Finished Dimensions 10"W x 62"L
8epi, 8ppi

Equipment
Loom with minimum 8" weaving width
8 dent reed
1 shuttle
Yarn ball winder and umbrella swift (or wind by hand)
Simple kitchen scale to weigh yarn if using a wind-along

Materials (see Yarn Advice p.X)**
A = 1 Skein Interlacements Yarns Michigan, 100% superwash merino in Indian Camp, 1100 yards (uses 230 yards).
B = 2 Skeins Hamilton Yarns, Sister Silk, 100% silk in Pine, 131 yards each (uses 203 yards).
C = 1 Skein Malabrigo Silkpaca, 70% baby alpaca & 30% silk in Teal Feather, to wind with A, 420 yards (uses 230 yards).

23

A = [1] SUPER FINE

B = [3] LIGHT

C = [0] LACE

The **materials list** will assign letters to the yarns used. <u>To avoid errors, it's a good idea to write the yarn names and colors that you choose beside their corresponding letter on charts that follow.</u> The yarns are given with the brand, fiber, put-up (weights in grams or ounces and yardage), and the actual yards used.

The **gauge** of each yarn is shown here.

Degree of Difficulty (adapted from the Craft Yarn Council)

Basic Projects using basic plain weave with simple warping and finishing.

Easy Projects may include minor variation of basic weave structures, yarn changes, and/or simple variations on warp technique or finish. May also include simple sewing.

Intermediate Projects may include multiple weave structures and/or require good sewing skills for construction.

Complex Projects may include multiple weave structures, complex patterning, challenging yarn combinations, and/or good sewing skills.

Reading Warp and Weaving Charts

	4x	
A'	B	A'
18		18
	2	

Charts for warping your loom, like the one at left, can be read from the right or the left. If you are right handed, start on the right. Left handers will probably choose to start on the left. This chart represents the number of ends (unless otherwise noted) that you will draw through the reed. As an example: If you are direct warping from the right, facing the back of the loom, tie on to the rod at the right side and draw 9 loops through consecutive slots to make 18 ends (every loop you pull is 2 ends). This will be color A' because it is under column A'. Next, draw 2 ends (1 loop) of B yarn (under column B). The grey box over the top of A' and B indicates 4 repeats of the A'-B sequence outlined in bold. You'll finish with 18 ends (9 loops) of A'.

Why don't charts give you the number of loops? Answer: because not everyone uses the direct warping technique dealing with loops. If using a warping board, you would be counting number of ends. **All the patterns in this book** **have been completed with a direct warp.**

Charts for weaving, like the one at right, are read from the top down. The letters over the top are the yarn selection. This chart tells you to weave 7" of C, then 17" of A, and so on, downward to completion. As mentioned previously, note your yarn selection next to their letters at the top, and you will avoid mistakes. You may see inches, number of picks, or number of repeats designated in each step in my weaving charts. This sequence may be repeated once or multiple times within a pattern.

A	C
	7"
17"	
	6"
17"	
	7"

Common Weaves (used in "Whip up a Bag" on p. 46)

On the next page, I give you brief descriptions of some very useful weaves for your reference. You'll need them to make the bag pattern and they're good to know regardless. You can find more detail on leno weave in my first book, *Woven Style for the 15" Rigid Heddle Loom*. Additionally, there are several good YouTube videos on these techniques and the hemstitching used in the bag swatch.

A. 3/1 Weft floats (weft is dominant; floats over 3 ends, under 1)

To set a pick-up stick to create an alternate shed:

Open a shed with heddle down. Working behind your reed with the pick-up stick, dip into the raised warp (upper row) and pick up the first and every other raised warp strand to place it on top of the stick. Push the pick-up stick flat and onto the back beam when not in use. For the Bag, follow the steps given in the box at right for your pick-up sequence. It is assumed, not stated, that you will throw the shuttle after you move the heddle in each step.

NOTE – YOU WILL NEED TO MANAGE EDGES AS YOU WORK THE FLOAT ROWS. If your weft does not catch the outer selvage thread, manually wrap your shuttle around it before throwing it into the shed. The location of these missed ends is determined by where you start your shuttle and the particular pick-up pattern. Once you determine where this will occur, it will happen in the same place on each repeat.

1.	Heddle up.
2.	Pick-up stick (put heddle in neutral and pull stick forward, placing it upward against heddle).
3.	Heddle up.
4.	Pick-up stick.
5.	Heddle up.
6.	Pick-up stick.
7.	Heddle up.
8.	Heddle down.

For B and C that follow, edges will tend to draw in where you let the weft rise for the open rows. Leave the weft at the edges loose, but not sloppy, and don't expect perfection at the selvages.

B. 2:2 Leno on an open shed (twisting 2 warp threads in holes with 2 warp threads in slots)

Open a shed so that the right outermost warp end is at the top. With the fingers of your left hand, pull the top right warp threads slightly to the left. With the pick-up stick, dip down and pick up the first 2 bottom warp threads, placing them onto the top of the stick. Drop 2 of the top warp threads from your left hand so that they snap to the underside of the stick. This crosses the ends, 2 by 2. Repeat this action across. To make sure you have not skipped any ends, pull the stick forward periodically to check that your crosses look consistent. If they don't, back up and redo the twist.

C

B

A

Next, turn the pick-up stick on edge, and push it away from you to make a special shed. Throw your shuttle through the shed, in front of the stick. Remove the stick and beat the weft for an even line that falls about 1/4"-1/2" away from previous pick. You can use the pick-up stick before removing to set the pick if preferred. The gap between picks creates a lacey, open effect. Change the shed (important) and weave a pick of plain weave. Beat this pick, leaving about 1/4"-1/2" gap as you did with pick #1. These 2 picks constitute one repeat of leno.

C. Brooks Bouquet on an open shed:

Open a shed, working from the right. Pass your shuttle into the shed and under 4 warp ends of the upper row (or the desired number of ends you want to bundle) and exit the shed through the top of your work. Bring the shuttle back into the shed, under the first 4 ends again and under 4 more ends of the upper row. Exit from the front. Cinch that first bundle tightly to form an hourglass shape. *Insert the shuttle into the shed where that bundle leaves off, go under 8 ends of the upper row, and exit through the front again, cinching the bundles surrounded as you go. Repeat from * across. Beat this pick 1/4"-1/2" above the previous pick. Change the shed and throw 1 pick of plain weave, beating to the same 1/4"-1/2" rise. This completes one repeat.

13

Equipment I Can't Live Without

Let's face it. We consume a lot of yarn! Since much of our yarn comes in hanks, or skeins as we tend to call them these days, my ball winder (1) and umbrella swift (2) get a good workout turning those skeins into usable balls.

My umbrella swift is mounted on the back of a chair with the shaft horizontal. This makes it easier to fight gravity with slippery skeins vs. a vertical mount where the shaft points up..

The basic kitchen scale (3), weighing both grams and ounces, is indispensable. If my label reads 109 yards in a 50 gm skein, I divide 109/50 to get the number of yards/gram (2.18 in this case). If I have just 20 grams left, 20 x 2.18 = 43.60 yards remaining.

Lastly, for power winding, I love my Winderfull (4). I use it along with my power drill. For the source, see p. 118.

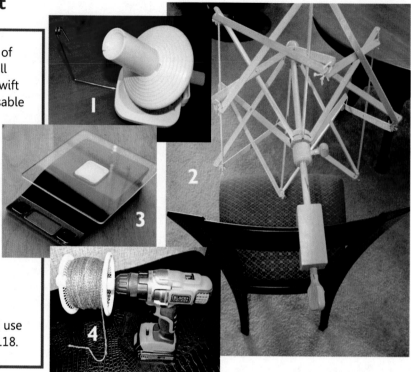

What is Assumed

Measurements: Weaving length is measured while the fabric is under tension on the loom for all patterns. Measurements given are generally rounded to the nearest 1/4".

Warping: My warp lengths assume direct warping and tying on with bows (rather than knots) in the front (my preference). Patterns requiring wider than 15" weaving width will have a couple extra inches included in warp length as the larger looms generally have greater depth and more waste. If you are using a larger loom for pieces narrower than 15", you may want to add 2" to the warp length just to be safe.

Weaving: It is presumed that you will weave a header before you begin weaving every time, so this in not mentioned within the patterns. I am in the habit of using scrap yarn of the same gauge or the actual weaving yarn with a piece of contrasting scrap in between to distinguish the header. The same gauge yarn will give you a better start.

My book, *Woven Style for the 15" Rigid Heddle Loom,* has advice on handling 2 shuttle weaving, picking up stitches for knitting, selvage improvement, and weaving terms to refine your skills in these areas if needed.

Fringe: Finished lengths exclude any fringe. The number of strands you use in tying your fringe tassels is a personal preference, so this is not always specified. I'm usually a 3-strand tassel girl unless the warp is very fine. Don't worry about the end count dividing evenly by the 3 strands. Just compensate with the strand count on 1 or 2 tassels if needed. I seldom do a finish twist my fringe as it is not a look I prefer, but feel free to do so if you like.

Washing: You will find that I recommend hand washing the woven pieces before sewing or before adding knitting or crochet to make the fabric more workable and accommodate shrinkage.

Sewing

In order to "go beyond the rectangle" you will need to do a little (mostly simple) sewing. This is a subject that makes some weavers a little nervous. The answer to anxiety here? Practice the finishing advice contained in this section with your scraps, test any cut edges thereafter by pulling at them with your fingers to determine how they withstand stress, and learn what to do if the cut warp ends escape the finish treatment. Furthermore, as is often said, measure twice, cut once. Once you do a lot of this, you will love altering handwoven fabrics into wearable and usable art!

Equipment: A simple, entry level machine that will do a straight and a zigzag stitch forward and backward will do, as long as it works well on multiple layers of thicker fabric. Use of a walking foot on your machine will help you move along on the extra bulk of handwoven material.

You will also need a good steam iron to set your seams as you sew. Be very aware of whether your yarn content includes synthetics. If so, you will need to go lightly at the lower steam settings and use a pressing cloth between the iron and the fabric or you may end up with melted fiber on your iron plate!

You will also need lots of straight pins, some good sharp scissors, a tape measure, and a sewing needle if hand stitching is needed. Locking stitch markers (like the kind knitters use) are also great for marking important points on the cloth.

It all Starts with the Raw Finish

Your first action before cutting will be to make sure that warp and weft ends are secured and won't unravel.

You can seal a cut edge with a serger, or by ironing a narrow piece of fusible interfacing at the cutting line. I'm on a mission to make our craft as accessible as possible without having to invest in a lot of expensive equipment, so my preferred method uses my sewing machine as described below. Regardless, you might like to try alternate methods on your scrap fabric to see how they work for you if you are curious.

You'll end by weaving a 1/2" footer of scrap yarn (same as a header but at the end). This protects the fabric from unraveling until you can get it to the sewing machine.

Adjust the stitch length and width to sew together the **2nd and 3rd pick** from the cutting edge. Start your sewing before the selvage and run the stitch off the other end to ensure that you've secured all warp ends. Two rows, one over the other or one just inside the other, normally does the trick unless I've specified otherwise. Where the raw finish edge gets lots of exposure, I will use 3 rows. Finish by **cutting along pick 1** to trim away excess material. This way you'll create a clean finish and avoid catching any header or footer scrap yarn in your stitching.

More Sewing Tips

With the limits of width and the weight of the fabric from our rigid heddle, a little creativity is called for to achieve wearable results. Because we can use our selvages as finished edges, minimal sewing is usually all we need. Most of the sewing required herein, takes a maximum of 1-2 hours (usually less) before you are done. What follows are a few basic tips for optimal results.

I will assume that you will backstitch lightly at the beginning and end of your seams to secure them so that is not mentioned in the instructions.

If you are unsure of yourself, use a long basting stitch (longest setting on your machine, may be 5-9mm) for testing. If that works, you can go back over it with a shorter stitch. I use a 3mm stitch length for most straight stitching as it holds, but will rip out easily if needed.

You will want to think about how you coordinate your sewing thread. I don't like a perfect match of thread to fabric because stitching easily disappears from view into the fabric. If you do have to rip out seams (mistakes happen and adjustments are sometimes necessary), a slightly contrasting thread can be very helpful.

In the creation of prototypes for designs, I have often abused my poor fabric with changes and adjustments. Your handmade fabric is probably more resilient than you think. On occasion however, a loose end sneaks out of the stitching with the kind of wear and tear I impose when designing. If stray unraveling happens to you, just take the piece back to the sewing machine for some over sewing with more zigzag stitch at that point.

Double fold, bias seam binding will be your friend for permanently sealing raw edges. Wide single fold can work but is harder to find. Occasionally, I turn the raw finished edge of the fabric inward and sew a 1/4" - 3/8" machine stitched hem without the binding. I call this a **raw finish hem**. Since you have zigzagged twice and then sewn a straight stitch to close the hem, this is still very secure, albeit more raw on this inside for what that matters.

This narrow, raw finish hem can be especially effective when hemming a curve.

It is unlikely that I will recommend a double fold hem (where you turn the edge once, then twice to sew it shut). The bulk that results from a double fold hem looks too stiff for my taste. I have, however, planned ahead on occasion and woven with sewing thread or a fine lace gauge yarn for 1" or so before proceeding with my regular weft. This creates a lighter weight start to the fabric to allow a double fold hem. Test this out when you are sampling to see if it suits you.

I've done my best to be scientific about the measurements in the garment patterns by testing and reviewing the results multiple times. Truthfully though, your weaving, draw-in, and shrinkage will be unique to you. I advise that you make a habit of frequent measuring of your pieces as you work to see if you are close to the size you've chosen (when it matters) or to modify to your own specifications. It helps to know some basic crochet or knit stitches when you want to add a little length or finish to your woven creation.

A word on picking up stitches: My method for picking up stitches to knit is to pull them up with a crochet hook at 2 ends below the selvage. If you use a hook without a handle, you can pick up 15-20 at a time, then just slide them off the back of the hook onto your knitting needle for speedy results. Mark increments of 4" on the fabric for periodic checking of stitch count.

Lastly, I recommend washing fabrics and seam bindings before sewing them together. They will be more workable. Also, with the shrinkage already accounted for, you can make adjustments more effectively. Bindings can be washed and dried in the washing machine.

I am not a master seamstress (or even close), so you can rest assured that I experienced a little anxiety of my own before I grew comfortable cutting into my weaving. If you are gifted at sewing, you may have even more inventive ideas to lend to our finish craft. Remember that **I love to hear your ideas!** If you would like to share them with my weaving community, contact me at www.poffstudio.com. I'll give you name mention if I use them in my work.

A Quick Trip Around the Color Wheel

If I had a nickel for every time I've heard, "I just don't have a sense for color" ...

While it's true that a few people have a wonderfully innate sense of color, a great many of us can benefit from a little structured advice for putting color choices together in our weaving. This chapter won't make you a scholar of color theory, but it will give you some help when heading to the yarn store, so take this book with you. I'll show you how to use it in the next few pages.

Ever since Sir Isaac Newton explored the bands of color in refracted beams of light, we have utilized the wheel like the RYB (red, yellow, blue) version below to convey the remarkable properties of color. The middle ring represents pure color. The outer ring shows each hue with some black added (referred to as a **shade**), and the inner ring has some white added (this is a **tint** of the hue). The term **tone** is used if gray is added.

The number 1's represent the **primary colors**, red, yellow, blue. When referring to visible light, these are the broadest bands of color in a beam of light. When all 3 are projected and overlapped, we have white light. Don't try this at home, by the way, it only works for light beams and not for paint, or yarn for the matter!

2's are **secondary** colors. These are the colors produced when two primaries are mixed. Notice they are half way between the primaries. 3's are **tertiary**: produced by combining a primary and a secondary.

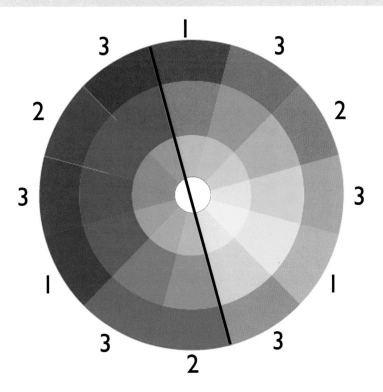

Color's 3 properties: **hue, value, and intensity,** are described as the color name, the lightness or darkness of the color, and the richness or dullness of the color respectively.

Hue

A pleasing combination of color is deemed **harmonious.** While harmony is an unsettled debate in color theory, **analogous** hues are easily defined as harmonious. These are the colors that are next to each other or close to each other on the wheel.

We know that the 12 colors on our wheel will not match the infinite range of hues available to us, but start with a decision as to which color your first yarn choice starts from. Is it closer to blue, like a blue-violet, or closer to red like a violet red? Then add hues that are within 1-2 steps, even up to 4 steps, <u>around</u> the wheel (before you get to another primary). There is your analogous color scheme.

As examples of analogous combinations, look at the shrug on p. 98 composed of analogous colors and tints, and at right, the green is about 2 steps from the blue on our wheel. Even with rich color, these analogous schemes usually radiate a sense of calm in their relationship to each other unlike the photo below right.

For high energy in your color choices, you might go for **complementary colors.** These are colors that fall directly across from each other on the wheel like the orange and blue here. When placed next to each other, they set off a vibration where they meet. Interestingly, when painters blend these together, complementary colors create a muddy brown - they negate each other's intensity.

Think about this in your weaving. You might alternate 1 pick of orange with 1 pick of blue, and likewise in the warp, creating a fabric with equal dots of each color. **Optical mixing,** which is what our eyes do when colors are placed very close to each other in small amounts like you just did can cause us to perceive them as blended together. This can leave us with a very dull fabric.

Conversely, using the 2 hues in your weaving in equal, large size blocks, will get you maximum excitement and a potentially gaudy fabric.

Now picture a pinstripe of orange plaid on a predominately blue sea. You get a vibrant result while applying some control to that combination. You gave one of the complements **dominance** over the other for an interesting fabric.

The multicolor yarn used in the shoulder cozy on p. 64 has flecks of complementary color, orange and blue, on a dominant neutral background to further demonstrate how controlling **proportion** of color can be effective.

If you are still with me, you might be sensing the importance of color relationships, which brings us to **simultaneous contrast**. Color can change noticeably based upon how you surround it. Take a close look at the gold balls of yarn in the photo at the bottom of this page. These are the same color and dye lot. Notice that the one in the middle of the orange yarn looks darker than the one surrounded by purple.

Hues also have relative **temperature**. Look back at our color wheel where I've drawn the line dividing the wheel in half. It's typical to refer to the right side of my line as *warm* and the left side as *cool*, with the tertiary colors (#3's) that border the line unclear as to which side of the line they should occupy. These can be considered neutral in temperature.

Looking again at the photo below, we can see an example that temperature is relative to its surroundings as well. The gold ball at right appears warmer next to the cool violet while the one at left appears to have been cooled or made more neutral by the warm orange. You can make one color look like two by surrounding it strategically.

Try This, It's Fun!

As a weaver, there's a good bet that you have a lot of odd balls of yarn laying around - the proverbial yarn stash.

Dump as many balls of yarn on your kitchen table that available stash and space will allow.

Open up the color wheel page and see how many complementary pairs (opposite each other) that you can put together from your yarns. Don't just go for the primaries. If you find a red-violet and yellow green pair, notice how they work together or against each other.

Next try to group a few 2-4 color analogous combinations (beside or close to each other around the wheel).

Lastly, if you have enough yarn, pick two balls of the same color. See if you can surround them to make the color shift like I did below.

Did you find some new color schemes to try? Not enough yarn? Invite some friends over with their yarn stash and make it a competition, or better yet, a yarn swap!

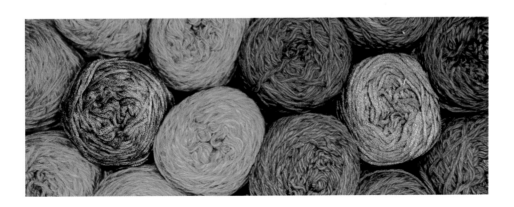

Value

Sometimes we get so caught up in beautiful colors, that we forget the importance of value in our choices. Below, I've pulled some colors from my yarns together and placed them in order of their value - the relative lightness or darkness they represent. Look at what happens when the photo is converted to black and white. We have 7 steps on the value scale.

Value advice: When it comes to color for weaving, you are likely to get happier results if you keep your values within 1 to 3 steps away from each other. As an example: combining colors with values #2 to #3 or #6 to #7 in our woven garments will generally be much more successful than putting a #1 value with a #7. Contrast adds interest, but high contrast values can disrupt the **unity** of the color design.

Hue is a major player, but don't forget value while you are at it! Note how a change in value of the weft in the scarf on p. 56 has a significant impact on the way the color projects in this piece.

p. 56

Try This!

As an extension of what we did in the last section, try grouping yarns from your yarn stash by their relative value. Squinting or taking black and white photos with your digital camera can help. This is a useful challenge to make you more aware of the way color's value affects your work.

Intensity

Intensity relates to a color's purity or **saturation**. The intensity of pure color can be lowered by the addition of black, white, gray or the color's complement. The color under #6 below is a pure blue with a rich intensity. The brown under #5 has a very low intensity compared to #6. More on intensity on p. 22– 23.

I   2   3   4   5   6   7

More About Color Combinations

Let's review and then expand our hue selection strategies. Back to the color wheel. We have names for certain combinations (illustrated below) that can help you make more conscious choices. You are, by now, familiar with the first 2, complementary and analogous. The black lines drawn on the wheels are drawn to intersect with colors that fit that named color combination.

For example, the line drawn horizontally on the first wheel runs through 3 analogous colors. The line drawn vertically on the next wheel links 2 complements. Moving right, the triangle and rectangle shapes touch the associated hues that qualify for the category noted underneath, along with the description and energy level normally associated with it.

Picture rotating the lines or shapes around the wheel and you will have numerous suggestions of color combinations that fit each strategy.

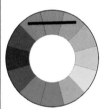    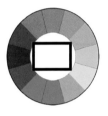 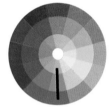

Analogous	Complementary	Triad	Spilt Complement	Tetrad	Monochromatic
Adjacent	Opposite	3 equidistant	1 primary, 2 tertiary	2 complementary pairs	shades/tints/tones of 1 hue
Calm	High Energy	High Energy	Med/High Energy	High Energy	Calm

Colors may be tinted, shaded or toned and proportions adjusted to modify energy levels.

Try It Online!

There are many free websites that allow you to trial color strategies online. At the writing of this book, there are 3 sites I like to play with: Plaidmaker.com will allow you to visualize color interplay, Adobe Color CC at https://color.adobe.com and an easy one you'll find from Sessions College at https://www.sessions.edu/color-calculator/ are great "color pickers".

If you prefer phone apps, you'll find dozens to play with. "Color Harmony" and "Color Mixer" are two of the many popular choices. You'll have ads if you want them for free.

Color evokes Emotion

...and symbolism which is influenced by culture. Here are some of the terms associated with colors. Note that they can be contradictory, depending on context.

Red - excitement, passion, joy, aggression
Orange - joy, warmth, happiness, freedom
Yellow - cheerfulness, optimism, intellect, fear
Blue - peace, coolness, sincerity, depression
Green - calm, nature, hope, envy
Purple and Violet - deep feeling, loyalty, luxury, death
Pink - playful, feminine, sensual, tranquil
Brown - dreary, earthy, grounding, honest
Beige - calm, relaxing, dependable, conservative

When I designed the cover poncho, I wanted this piece to glow with warmth, joy, and excitement; hence my choice of reds and oranges. Also note that the gradient colors of red to orange are analogous. In this example the intensity and emotions associated with the colors take dominance over the calm tendency we look for in analogous combinations.

What feelings do you want to communicate in your work?

A Tale of 2 Scarves, Contrast, Reinforcement, and Intensity

At right, I've photographed 2 scarves next to each other. These were created on one warp. The painted or palindrome warp technique used is detailed in my book, *Woven Style for the 15" Rigid Heddle Loom*. This involves symmetrically dyed skeins that are laid out so that the color repetitions pool together. I've aligned the scarves to allow the warp colors to match across both pieces so you can see the differing effect of a black vs. light interweave.

With the first scarf, I used a black weft. The 2nd uses a light green weft. I show a little of the fringe at top left and bottom right for each scarf so you can see the actual warp colors at those edges.

While the light green weft on light green warp **reinforces** the color at top right, retaining its intensity, this weft tends to mute the colors as you look further down toward the purple transition. The lighter color is **tinting** the other colors and reducing their intensity. The black weft at left is **shading** the colors, but provides **contrast** and makes that purple warp richer.

Try using a black weft to enrich a warp that starts out a little dull in color.

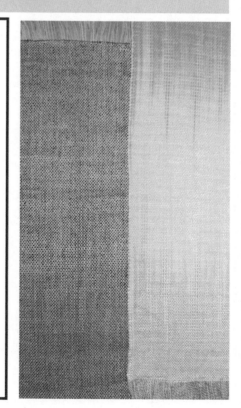

Proportion

Now we get into the mathematical part of our color conversation. That sentence alone is likely to cause a chorus of groans from most of my students. If you are following a pattern, this is not something you have to be concerned with. If you want to do a little designing of your own though, you can get through this element with intuition and a few guidelines.

1. Color schemes work best when amounts of color are not equal.

2. Your boldest brightest colors will leap forward and grab attention. Think about using smaller amounts of them in your design to keep your work from shouting at you (unless that is your goal).

3. Keep your eyes open for how others have used color in various proportions that please you (fabrics, paintings, photos).

For my math lovers, there are many mathematical theories for color proportion. One easy one is the basic 60:30:10 rule for 3 color themes. Chose a color to represent 60% of your overall design, then a 2nd color that will be 30% and wind up with an accent at 10% of the total.

Or you may have heard about the Fibonacci Sequence which is a sequence of numbers where each number is the sum of the previous 2 numbers, i.e. 0, 1, 1, 2, 3, 5, 8, 13, and so on to infinity. The relationship of these numbers converges on a ratio (the Golden Ratio, 1:1.618) that appears to organize many formations in nature from seed pods to galaxies. It's probably no surprise then, that we find this ratio pleasing.

Here's what you do, Fibonacci fans. Plan your color proportions to coincide with contiguous numbers on the sequence. Example: 2" stripe, 3" stripe, 5" stripe. You selected the 3 numbers I underlined on the series above. You can apply this to stripes, warp threads, color blocks, oh boy!

You can also try the Lucas series (another mathematician). This is a sequence with the same progression as Fibonacci, but starts with 2, 1, rather than 0, 1. Here it is: 2, 1, 3, 4, 7, 11, 18...

Putting it Together - Composing Your Color Story

What we want to achieve in our work is harmony (a pleasing color combination) and **unity** - and maybe a certain emotion as well. Unity is the sense that the elements (including hue, value, intensity, temperature, contrast, and proportion) pull together in the final piece.

If all of this is a little daunting, don't forget that your intuition is still key to choosing colors, knowledge is supportive to intuition, and rules are made to be broken! So start with colors that you like. If that works for your senses, then you are done. Otherwise go back to the topics in this section and see where some conscious application of advice will help you jazz it up a bit.

As an example: If your choices don't create sufficient contrast to make them interesting, think about giving **dominance** to an element. The cowl on p. 45 shows mostly low intensity colors. The temperature change of the hot red moves forward keeping this one from being dull.

Try This!

This is a good time to go back through some of your past projects and analyze color choices you have made, both successful and unsuccessful. Try to determine what color schemes they may compare to.

The idea is to become more aware to gain control over the outcome of your projects.

A Word About Neutrals

There is a cleanliness and simplicity to working with gray, black, and white (achromatic, meaning without color) as well as neutral shades, tints, and tones. The key to choosing this strategy with wearables is to understand how these neutrals work with your skin and your preferences. Neutrals can be a challenge to many skin tones. Loads of information can be found on the internet to determine the best clothing colors for your coloration. I recommend that you look into this research if you are going to pursue garment weaving.

In working with achromatic and neutrals, take another look at p. 20. Your neutrals can be warm like the skein under #5, vs. cool like its achromatic counterpart beneath. You'll want to consider if your choices will radiate warmth or if you prefer to coordinate cool shades. Perhaps you can get away with a contrast of warm and cool as I have done below right. The introduction of a singular color with achromatic black can make a more striking statement than the stark contrast of black and white.

This singular color enhancement makes neutrals compatible with more skin tones. The black and white cowl on p. 39, with overtones of green, follows this strategy.

By the way, emotionally speaking, black is associated with power, fear, sophistication, and death. White conveys purity, innocence, light, and goodness,

...and Multicolor Yarns

We have such a wonderful array of multicolor yarns available to us, both commercially prepared and hand dyed, to produce colorful results in our weaving. With these yarns, the dye master has decided most of the color scheme for us. To get the maximum out of multis, I generally choose black or a solid or tonal color addition that picks up a dominant color in the multi. Adding some textured yarns like a faux fur as in the top on p. 88 or a ribbon can make a nice companion, but it's a good idea to keep the novelty a solid or semi-solid hue to avoid competition with all that color. You will want to give some thought as to whether you want your multicolor yarn to run vertically or horizontally. More on this on p. 37.

"What can I weave with?"

...the number one question I am asked.

The short answer is "Everything in the yarn shop with a few considerations".

Specific to selecting a warp, you will have to keep in mind the gauge (how it will perform with

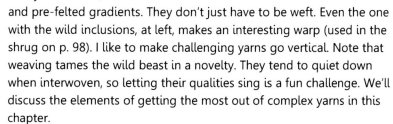

the reed size), the tensile strength (will it hold up to the tension of my loom), and the elasticity. Your weft, on the other hand, can be almost anything because we don't have the concerns about tension and reed size. When putting them together, besides thinking about how it will look, you will need to consider the drape, weight, how it feels on your body, and durability. Will your garment have to stand up to frequent washing or winter weather?

At right, are some of the yarns I've used in the patterns in this book: ribbon, chunkies, slub yarn, bouclé,

and pre-felted gradients. They don't just have to be weft. Even the one with the wild inclusions, at left, makes an interesting warp (used in the shrug on p. 98). I like to make challenging yarns go vertical. Note that weaving tames the wild beast in a novelty. They tend to quiet down when interwoven, so letting their qualities sing is a fun challenge. We'll discuss the elements of getting the most out of complex yarns in this chapter.

Fiber

You might be one of those lucky folks who can wear a scratchy mohair next to your skin with ease. You might be ok with some super fine merino or alpaca next to your skin. Superwash wool, where the natural scales of the fiber flatten a bit may work for you, or you might be like me. Even some cotton textures can feel scratchy around my neck. I love animal fibers for weaving, but those microscopic barbs on the ends that make them so great for hand spinning drive me up a wall, even from the finest animal hair. However, I can consider them for outerwear. The cover piece was woven with a substantial amount of wool, but the collar has a strategic blend of cotton, bamboo, silk and elastic nylon to keep my sensitive neck happy!

Decide how you are going to use the fabric and, especially if you are like me, be very mindful of what's going into your weaving. Let's break that down on the next page.

25

To be a better garment weaver...

Become a label reader

When it comes to fiber choices, there are a multitude of varieties and blends to choose from. For you to be an astute label reader, I've compiled the following "pocket guide" to commonly used yarns.

For wearable fabric, you'll want to decide the degree of warmth, **absorbency** (for moisture release to keep you comfortable), softness, **elasticity** (for shape retention), and weight that you desire.

Here are the main categories of fiber, how some of their members reflect the above qualities, and my approach for using them.

Protein Fibers are grown on an animal or extruded

from a critter (silk from the silkworm). These yarns are absorbent and good insulators for warmth. When it comes to choosing them for garment weaving, the animal fibers with a finer diameter are the best choices. These fibers are made up of scales that **felt** (bond) together under heat and abrasion - except for silk. This makes the yarns expand and **full** (to bloom and become thicker).

Wool - If your skin likes animal fibers, wool is light weight, flame retardant, and resilient. One of my favorites for its softness is Merino wool. Its finer fiber diameter gives it a great **hand** (feel).

Peruvian Highland wool is commonly found in reasonably priced classics. This is a cross between Corriedale and Merino sheep and works well for outerwear for its long, strong, yet soft nature.

Wool can be treated to resist bloom (called superwash). This removes or coats the scales. Superwash can be easier on the skin, but less desirable if you want your fabric to full.

Cashmere (from cashmere goats) is known for its super soft, luxurious fiber and high price. Not as elastic, but warmer and lighter than wool. Quality blends will simulate the softness and keep the price down. Beware of low-end blends that may include insignificant amounts of cashmere, have undesirable guard hairs, or are too loosely spun to hold together.

Angora comes from angora rabbits and is another luxury fiber also lighter and warmer than wool, Angora has very little crimp, and therefore not a lot of elasticity, so don't expect it to hold its shape over time. Blending with a soft wool can make this more desirable for weaving.

Alpaca is absorbent, lustrous, and soft. It doesn't have the lanolin that wool has, so it's cleaner and may be better for those with a wool allergy. Warmer than wool, its hollow fiber insulates against the cold. It is also more dense and heavier. Super fine and baby alpaca provide the softest results. Check the spin on your Alpaca to see if it holds up to tension and abrasion.

Mohair comes from angora goats, not to be confused with angora rabbits. While this yarn tends to be scratchy, kid mohair (from younger goats) is softer, especially when combined with silk. You find it in the shops as bouclé (loops) when wound around a nylon binder thread. These loops may then be brushed to create the hairy stuff we are used to. Nonbrushed without the nylon core is smoother, but hard to find. Mohair's surface is lustrous, reflecting color beautifully. Use a wide sett for brushed (8 dent for even the finest gauges) as it is "sticky" (p. 30), beat lightly for an open weave, and shock it in a hot water bath to stabilize it if needed. Mohair is not the first yarn choice for beginners.

COLOR 62305

DYE LOT 7A6744

3.5 oz · 100 g
215 yds · 198 m

50% Super Fine Alpaca
Alpaga Super Fin
50% Peruvian Wool
Laine Péruvienne

For best results, alternate knitting from two different hanks every 2 to 4 rows.

knitting gauge
5 sts = 1"
5 mm
8 US
20 sts
4", 10 cm
26 Rows

crochet gauge
4 sc = 1"
5 mm
8(H) US
16 sc
4", 10 cm
22 Rows

4 MEDIUM

Silk, which doesn't have the scales of other protein fibers, is the cocoon of the silkworm. It's one of the strongest fibers with very little give in the weaving (stretches later in the wearing). Due to its delayed elasticity, we can often use a finer gauge at a wider set than expected and still get stable fabric. Great drape and openness results. It displays color richly, absorbs moisture like wool, and blends well with other fibers.

You'll see bombyx or mulberry silk, named after what the worm eats, in 3 grades: reeled which is the highest, spun which is more textural, and bourette (silk noils) which is not as shiny and is nubby. Then there is tussah or wild silk (not commercially cultivated) which can be shinier and more slippery (unless it is of the bourette or noil grade) which may make it harder to weave by itself. You commonly find tussah working beautifully in blends.

Cellulose Fibers

are derived from the seed pods (like cotton) or the stalks (like linen and hemp) of plants.

Cotton - is strong, breathable, and easy next to the skin. It can be mercerized which is a processing that increases luster and smoothness (think perle cotton), but I generally find it too stiff for wearable fabric.

Among the varieties, Egyptian and Pima cotton are the highest quality with their long fibers. You won't find much elasticity in a pure cotton, but an unmercerized, organic cotton would be my first choice for the few times I use 100% cotton for garments as it tends to be softer, retain a hint of elasticity, and is eco-friendlier. Otherwise, I prefer my cotton in blends.

There's not a lot of warmth in cotton, but unmercerized will be slightly warmer.

Linen, stronger than cotton, also lacking in elasticity, can be rather stiff for weaving garments if you are looking for soft. Linen will usually soften in the wash and in the wearing over time, but weavers get less of the benefit of drape than knitters are accustomed to. If you want a crispness to your piece, though, linen will give it to you. It also has a wonderful moisture wicking quality for warm weather comfort.

Hemp is a sustainable, eco-friendly fiber that weaves up much like linen, but don't expect it to soften as quickly. However, it can be awesome for making open, airy shawls where the crispness contributes to a unique fabric.

Semi-Synthetic (Cellulosic) Fibers

are from plant material chemically processed and extruded into a fiber. These are most often rayon or viscose (named for the process). The labels are essentially interchangeable, although rayon uses cellulose from a variety of plants (bamboo, soy, etc.) while viscose comes from wood pulp or cotton linter (young fibers close to the seed).

These yarns have earned the name "artificial silk" because they take dye easily, are silky soft, and have a lustrous quality; great for sensitive skin. Cellulosic fibers are absorbent, but fragile when wet, so handle with care until dry. Rayon and viscose tend to "grow" or stretch over time and have little memory. Also, the fabric of pure rayon can have considerable weight. This makes for great drape, but here is where it pays to understand the fiber's capabilities in case you are looking for something lighter weight with more retention.

Although the sources are generally sustainable, there is much debate about the highly chemical path of these fibers. On the bright side, we are seeing manufacturers work towards less toxic processes, and more recycled versions are appearing. Rayon's newer family member, lyocell (Tencel is the brand name in the US, therefore capitalized) is a step forward in eco-friendly production.

Synthetics

include acrylic, polyester, and nylon (a.k.a. polyamide), Synthetics are entirely manmade from chemicals, You see them frequently as an add-in to other fibers for many reasons. Synthetics can lend softness, strength, and retention to a blend.

On the negative side, synthetics are subject to pilling, flammability, and melting under a hot iron. Also, they lack breathability unless produced as a microfiber. I find them undesirably "crunchy" to the hand. For these reasons, and because they are made from petroleum products or coal, I generally prefer to keep synthetics to a minimum.

Blends

Get to know the strengths and weaknesses of each category of fiber. Manufacturers create blends to capture the better features of fibers to alter the yarn's performance. Blends therefore, can make for some superior weaving yarns.

Being a label reader armed with the knowledge of fiber content and performance will take you a long way toward more predictable results in your weaving.

Yarn Gauge and Sett - Fabric Stability

Notice the wavy lines in the fabric at right? Sometimes you see this as you weave or where the fabric rolls over the tension beam on certain looms or not until the weaving is removed from the loom. This was the result of a slippery warp too fine for the reed size used. This caused the weft to shift and bunch together - an example of unstable fabric. As I often say, there is a happy place between a stiff fabric and an unstable one. Getting it right is a matter of knowledge, experience, and lots of testing.

P.S. We might live with a little of this instability as I did with my lace scarf here. The goal is to minimize it.

Gauge for Label Readers.

Circled below are standard symbols for knitting yarns. You read the rectangular diagrams as:

Left: 20 stitches (sts) over a 4-inch (10cm) swatch on a US 8 (5mm) knitting needle OR 16 single crochet (sc) over that swatch on a US 8 (H) or 5mm crochet hook. These details coincide with a Craft Yarn Council #4 as seen on the next page. You may not see both indicators on a label, so it helps to become familiar with each reference to know what gauge yarn you have.

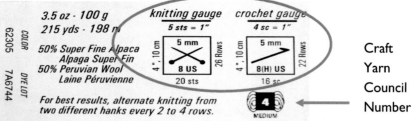

Craft
Yarn
Council
Number

Knitting Yarns

Yarn Weight Symbol & Category Names	0 LACE	1 SUPER FINE	2 FINE	3 LIGHT	4 MEDIUM	5 BULKY	6 SUPER BULKY	7 JUMBO
Categories of yarn, gauge ranges, and recommended needle and hook sizes								
Type of Yarns in Category	Fingering, 10 count crochet thread	Sock, Fingering, Baby	Sport, Baby	DK, Light Worsted	Worsted, Afghan, Aran	Chunky, Craft, Rug	Bulky, Roving	Jumbo, Roving
Knit Gauge Range* in Stockinette Stitch to 4 inches	33–40** sts	27–32 sts	23–26 sts	21–24 sts	16–20 sts	12–15 sts	7–11 sts	6 sts and fewer

Weaving Yarns

Cotton, Rayon weights

8/2   6/2-5/2   3/2

I've placed a few common weaving yarn weights under a corresponding category for knitting yarns above. You don't see knitting and weaving yarns cross referenced very often since these systems were not created with each other in mind!

Yarn weight for knitters is about categorizing a range of yarns by diameter and how they perform on different size needles, so weight actually refers to gauge here. Knitting yarns tend to be softer than weaving or cone yarns as they generally have less spinning oil in them and may be more loosely plied.

The weaving yarn numbering system is, more accurately, a weight reference. It starts with yards per pound. Established in the 19th century, a base standard for a single strand of cotton was set at 840 yards per pound as the #1. From there #2 is 1680 yds/lb (twice the yardage), #3 is 2520 yds/lb (3 times the yardage), and so on. This standard was also applied to rayon and its subcategories, such as lyocell (Tencel) and bamboo. The larger the number, the more yards in a pound, and the finer the strand. This weight is normally the first number in the pair. The 2nd is the number of plies.

Wool and other animal fibers, linen, and some types of silk each have their own standard, which adds to the complexity.

Throw blends into the equation, and the fact that some manufacturers will reverse the numbering system, and you can see that this can be a bit mind boggling. Additional detail on weaving yarns is outside the scope of this book, and generally outside what is useful for garment weaving on the rigid heddle (unless you want to double the finer yarns or use them as weft for a lighter weight fabric).

I sometimes choose cone yarns for plant-based fibers when I want a lighter weight, smooth thread to mix in with my knitting yarns, either as warp or weft, They play a suitable role in the background to lessen the weight of a fabric. They may also be more economical, and lighter gauge plant fibers can be harder to find among knitting yarns. Otherwise, I tend to leave the cone yarns to those who focus on producing home goods, tapestries, and functional items where larger quantities, stronger plies, and more bodied fabric are desirable.

Warp Sett, Standards and Deviations

Getting the reed size right is one of our great challenges. As you grow your skills, matching dent to yarn will be more obvious. Still, there are times when the assumptions of even the most experienced turn out wrong.

The first few inches of your weaving should be examined to determine if the fabric has stability and is what you intended. If you have the wrong reed, don't be afraid to unravel, untie, and transfer the warp to a different one. Unweaving is substantially faster than weaving! My YouTube video, "Rescues for Rigid Heddle Weavers", demonstrates a way to transfer the ends safely, as they must be kept in order when you do this.

For garment creation, I keep an eye on stability but strive to keep some "air in there" as well. I want to avoid beating too tightly and winding up with the equivalent of a gunny sack in the end. Balance, where the warp sett is close to the number of weft picks, is sought after for great drape. If you have an 8 dent reed, beating to 8 picks per inch is balanced. Even if you come close, say 8 epi (ends per inch) x 12 ppi (picks per inch), you are probably still going to get good drape with a soft yarn.

The word "beat" is often a misnomer when your real intention might be a "loving tap" to place one pick close to the other. Further, I advise against beating the same pick multiple times because you are more likely to create stiff fabric and frowning edges (selvages that sink when beating from various directions).

For reed size, the way we look at matching knitting gauge yarns to reed size is typically:

Sticky Warp

Woolen spun wools

Slubs & other textures

Mohair

Resistant Warp

Linen

Hemp

Cotton

Silk

Slippery Warp

Worsted spun wools

Cashmere

Alpaca

Rayon and its subcategories*

Not so fast though. I like to put warp yarns in 3 general categories for beat. First is sticky yarn. This can be a wool that is woolen spun: prepared and spun from fibers of different lengths, going in different directions. Textured yarns create a drag on your weft to slow down the beat and allow a wider sett.

Yarns with no or low elasticity are resistant to the beat like cellulose fibers or many silk varieties.

Then we have slippery yarns such as worsted spun (not to be confused with worsted gauge) which are smooth, same length fibers, prepared to go in the same direction. Since worsted or woolen spun are not normally on the label, you'll have to use your sense of touch to judge.

Looking at the small incremental difference between 8, 10, and 12 dent reeds, I consider the 10 dent "the middle guy" to put more air into the fabric of sticky or resistant sport gauge yarns or to stabilize and tighten slippery worsted gauge yarns.

12 dent - sock, sport, (some lace if it is sticky or resistant)

10 dent - dk

8 dent - worsted, aran (I use many dk yarns at this sett)

5 dent - chunky, bulky, super bulky if it fits

*rayon can be resistant when tightly plied due to its delayed elasticity, but its slick surface is slippery when loosely plied as with most rayon in knitting yarns. As always, sample, sample, sample. I have a YouTube video for that too! It's "Test Warp on the Rigid Heddle Loom".

Textures

Consider incorporating some of the novelty or complex textures that follow for one-of-a-kind wearables. A few thoughts on use.

1. Remember that weaving tends to refine even the wildest of textured yarns.

2. Warp: As always, make sure it passes the warp test, p. 10. Also, the thickest parts must pass easily through the heddle holes. Sometimes it helps to sley all the novelty ends through holes and put a smooth, non-woolly yarn in the slots between to help the warp do its up and down thing without sticking. In the case of the collar piece for the shrug on p. 98, the thick pieces were too much for the holes but handled fine through the slots, so I reversed this strategy putting smooth yarn in the holes.

3. If challenging the weaving capacity of the rigid heddle by warping with really exotic yarn, create pieces that are narrow for easier weaving. I did this with the abovementioned shrug piece. The wider the piece, the harder it can be to open a clean shed with "sticky" textured novelties.

4. I often interweave with a fine gauge weft, so it will recede and let the novelty show off. Don't expect the weft to travel straight across for a perfect fell line when there is lots of texture. You can use a fork, a tapestry beater, or a hair pick to straighten the weft that catches on inclusions and slubs. Be satisfied to let the weft meander across in this case as it may have to do (see photo, far right on p. 32).

Beaded or Sequined

Usually best as weft. If the beads or sequins are tiny and embedded well, this can be warp. Great as an accent to plain yarns.

Core Spun

A core yarn is wrapped by another thread. May have fibers protruding for added texture. Usually strong with a degree of elasticity.

Boucle

Loops made around a base yarn. See Magic Ball, p. 44 - 45. Use as warp or weft for surface texture. Sticky yarn that needs space. If warp, try smooth yarns between.

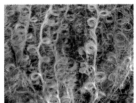

Corkscrew

One of two plies is spun at a different tension to make a corkscrew around the other ply.

Chenille

Very soft and fuzzy. Big Chenille p. 68. Formed with tufts of pile at right angles to a core yarn. Best in a tight sett for consistency.

Eyelash

Polyester or nylon with hairs evenly spaced that look like eyelashes. Prism Cool Stuff, p. 43, has elements of eyelash.

Crepe

The twist is tightened in places to give it a kink. Interlacements ZigZag, p. 68.

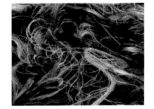

Faux Fur

Add more hair than Eyelash and you get fur. Good faux fur can be pricey, but it is a fun luxury to add elegance to a piece. Prism Plumette, p. 78 - 79.

Ladder

A tricky yarn for knitting, but it weaves easily as warp or weft. It is strong and gives a lacey effect. This yarn resembles a ladder with 2 threads that look like side rails and bits of color as rungs in between.

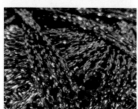

Metallic

Great if you love a little "bling". May be scratchy next to the skin.

Nub

A core thread that has nubs twisted into it. Flag yarn is a nub. Nub yarn does well as a contrast in an open weave with fine gauge yarns and mohair.

Ribbon

Synthetic or natural fibers that resemble a ribbon. Tape yarns are related, but they are flatter and more consistent like tape. Prism Tencel Tape, p. 78. I don't bother trying to keep these yarns flat as some weavers do. I don't find the twists and turns noticeable in the finished fabric.

Slub

Woven with thick and thin spots like the handspun on p. 46. Slub yarns need a sett wide enough to accommodate the thickest slub in the yarn.

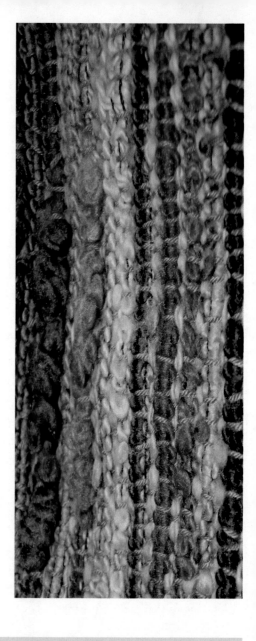

By giving thought to our wonderful range of yarns, I'm hoping that you will be inspired to get more creative with them. I recommend that you take time to trial these in swatches and keep good notes! For an idea of what to do with your swatches, see p. 46.

Notes on Elasticity

We've already covered the relative elasticity of different categories of yarns. Some yarns actually have elastic in their fiber content for noticeable additional stretch.

It's important for weavers to be aware of the element of elasticity when combining yarns. When the difference is dramatic in the <u>warp</u>, you may find significant puckering upon removal from the loom. Also, it may be difficult to get a clean shed opening. If there is a variation of stretch in the <u>weft</u>, you can have problems with different amounts of draw-in and wavy selvages as a result.

Unless you intend to gather your fabric, plan to combine similar levels of stretch (and shrinkage) in your warp. I'll show you how to deviate from that rule on p. 56.

Yarns with elastic content will need to be handled with a little extra allowance for the fabric to contract to its natural state.

The Patterns

Master Multicolored Yarns and Make Fragile Yarn go Vertical!

I fell in love with Interlacement's multicolored, hand dyed, superwash wool and immediately envisioned it elongated as warp. When I got it home and did the warp test, p. 10, however, I was surprised to find that it might not be strong enough to hold up to my loom's tension. Not to be discouraged, I made this scarf to show what I do to make fragile yarns work in the warp (and I had enough left over for another project from this big skein).

The combination of merino and silk makes this a super soft scarf with excellent drape.

Degree of Difficulty: Easy

Details on this challenge: Since we don't normally get to test the strength of a yarn before we buy it, use this advice when your warp selection breaks too easily, and you don't want to change your plans for it. If your warp is strong enough and it's a fingering gauge, you won't need to add the Malabrigo, yarn C, as a **wind-along**. In this case, adjust the reed to a 12 dent for fingering gauge, and you'll use a total of 368 yards of A instead.

Approximate Finished Dimensions 10" W x 60" L

8epi, 9-10 ppi

Equipment

Loom with minimum 13" weaving width

8 dent reed

1 shuttle

Yarn ball winder and umbrella swift (or wind by hand)

Simple kitchen scale to weigh yarn if using a wind-along to reinforce warp

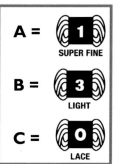

A = 1 SUPER FINE

B = 3 LIGHT

C = 0 LACE

Materials (see Yarn Advice p. 37 for additional selection information)

A = 1 Skein Interlacements Yarns Michigan, 100% superwash merino in Chairman of the Board, 8 oz = 1100 yds (uses 230 yards).

B = 2 Skeins Hamilton Yarns, Sister Silk, 100% silk in Pine, 50 gm = 131 yards each (uses 253 yards).

C = 1 Skein Malabrigo Silkpaca, 70% baby alpaca, 30% silk in Teal Feather, to wind with A, 50 gm = 420 yds (uses 230 yards).

At right, you can see the contrast between focusing this yarn warpwise (1) vs. weftwise (2). The long run gives a more scattershot color effect. Used the short way as weft, multicolors will pool together and translate as stripes. Further, using a multicolor as both weft and warp (3) will diffuse the color changes for lower contrast. I've used this in the sleeves of the sweatshirt on p. 68.

The silk yarn used as weft (B) in our project is a hand dyed tonal (a single color with a range of light to darker shades). This breaks the vertical striping up in a subtle way as you can see in the horizontal dark flecks in (1). I've reinforced that vertical look in the warp by adding a periodic stripe of the silk between every 18 ends of A.

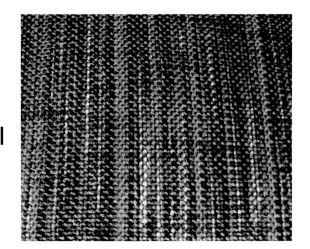

I

Yarn Advice

Adding a wind-along works best using animal fibers like wool or alpaca that are "sticky", p 30. They will hold together better. I have used rayon or Tencel as wind-alongs, but it is challenging to get them to work together as one because they are slipperier. If you are a spinner, you can ply them together on your wheel or spindle.

Prepare Double Strands:

To set up the wind-along, grab your kitchen scale and ball winder. Wind separate balls of A and C. Tie an end of each ball together so you can wind them as one. You will need a resulting ball of double stranded yarn that weighs around 80 grams (2-7/8 oz) for sufficient yardage.

How do I wind this weight? Since my ball winder weighs 233 gm (8-1/4 oz), I hold the winder in hand while I wind and weigh it periodically until the total of yarn and winder is 313 gm (11-1/8 oz).

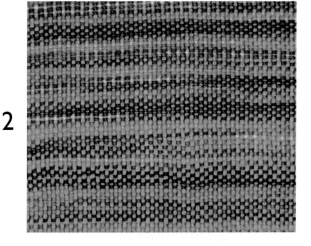

2

Warp with A' and B, 12-1/4" wide x 92" long (98 ends) according to the chart at right. A' is your new, double strand ball. Use A for A' if not using the wind-along. In this case, if you switched to the 12 dent reed, repeat the A-B sequence 6 times and end with the 18 ends of A. Warp width will be 11-1/2". See p. 12 if you need chart reading help.

	4x	
A'	B	A'
18		18
	2	

Weave 68" in plain weave with B.

Finish

Remove from the loom tying fringe with overhand knots. Hand wash with mild detergent in room temperature water and hang dry. Trim any hanging tails flush and cut the fringe to the desired length.

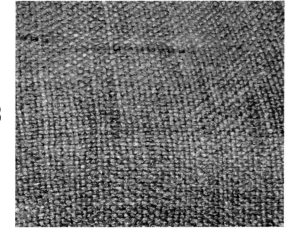

3

Whip up a Cowl and Make the Most of Hand Tied Yarns!

Finding novelty yarns is a little harder these days than it was a few years ago, and yet, these yarns are just so exciting for our work! Weaving has a way of taming even the wildest of knitting yarns. One way to get a mixed flock of fun textures, is to let a company like Prism Yarns put them together for you.

Prism's Stuff is featured in two colorways here. Unique textures, dyed in coordinating colors, will make you look like a wizard of weaving with just one skein!

The secret to showing off these hand tied novelty yarns lies in selecting the right warp and giving them a little space. For clues, read on...

Whip up a quick masterpiece today, wash it tonight, and wear it (or gift it) tomorrow! I love this open look cowl for all-weather wear. I add a little extra twist to the drape of this piece by ruching it at the shoulder. See the close-up, p. 42.

Degree of Difficulty: Easy

Details on this challenge: This is a simple, but rewarding, project. There are just a few tips to get the most from your complex textures used as weft. See the yarn advice on the next page.

Approximate Finished Dimensions: 12-1.2" W x 40" L
12epi, 9-12 ppi (varies as the yarn changes). Beat moderately, not hard.

Equipment
Loom with minimum 13" weaving width
12 dent reed
2 shuttles

A = 4 MEDIUM

B = 1 SUPER FINE

Materials (see Yarn Advice p. 42)

A = 1 skein Prism Cool Stuff Half, rayon, cotton, nylon, polyester, bamboo, Tencel, silk in Sedona for the lighter version OR 1 skein Prism Layers Stuff Half, rayon, cotton, nylon, kid mohair, bamboo, Tencel, wool, cashmere, and silk in Bracken for the darker version, 150 yards. (uses 90 yards).

B = uses 408 yards of fingering gauge yarn. A heavy lace gauge will work if using a yarn with less "give" like Tencel or silk. I used Prism Delicato Layers, 100% Tencel, in Begonia, 4 oz = 630 yards, for the lighter version and Berroco Cotton Comfort Sock, 50% nylon & 50% acrylic in Liquorice, 50 gm = 450 yards, for the darker version.

Yarn Advice

I usually select a solid warp color (or a subtle tonal) that will take a background role in the piece. I recommend that this warp color match one of the main colors in A. Alternatively, you can make a bold statement with black to heighten the color intensity.

Our novelty yarn, A, needs a little separation to show best, so I will have you alternate a pick of our solid color B with a pick of A to establish this spacing. Keeping the warp sett close and sandwiching the fancy yarn with the solid as you weave will bring more attention to this yarn's unique character.

The Prism Stuff yarns are very well gauge matched to help you keep your edges even. If you add other yarns, be aware that varying the yarn gauges will likely result in different amounts of draw-in and take-up that can make your selvages a little wavy (uneven).

You'll have plenty of yarn from this skein, so feel free to edit out textures or colors that you may want to minimize.

Warp with B, 14" wide x 68" long (168 ends).

Weave 44" in plain weave alternating 1 pick of A with 1 pick of B. End with 1 pick of A. When you come to a knot at the yarn change, you can either leave it showing in the fabric or cut it out and restart your weaving to trim the ends later as I did.

Finish

Remove from the loom, tying fringe with overhand knots.

Ruching: Locate a loop of weft at one selvage, midpoint between the ends of the scarf. Pull this loop from the edge to gather the fabric until its width is drawn down to 4" (see right). Cut the loop and tie the cut threads close to the fabric edge with a double knot to secure the gather. Weave the cut weft ends back into the fabric.

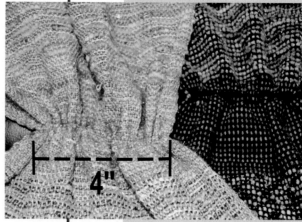

Wash with mild detergent in room temperature water and hang dry. Trim hanging tails flush and cut the fringe to the desired length.

To wear, place the ruched center on one shoulder or at back neck. Drape one fringed end over the other and a insert shawl pin through both layers.

In the cowl at right, I liked the contrast of the header scrap yarn so much that I decided to leave it in as you might notice at the edge. Experiment with what you like!

...or Make Use of Your Yarn Stash!

The cowl at right was made with 2 skeins of Be Sweet's Magic Ball (color Shakespeare) which was full of coordinating yarns of various fibers tied together in one skein. The yarns in these skeins are exotic and fun. You can get by with 1 skein and about 35 yards of scrap yarn you may have on hand...or you might want to make this completely from yarns you have stashed away. Start by pulling out the most interesting remnants you can find and group them together by colors that seem to work together. Next, locate a solid warp base that will either blend in with or deepen those colors using black or a dark coordinating color. See the section about color, p. 17 - 24, for guidance.

You can apply the principles of the previous cowl where we use a finer yarn for the warp at a close sett of 12 epi and then alternate weft picks of your textured yarn with this warp choice. This will give you a lighter weight fabric than the one shown at right. For my stash buster, I chose a warp yarn of sticky, 2 ply handspun that was dk to worsted gauge, set closely on a 10 dent reed. The tight sett created enough resistance to allow the warp to show through at about 8 ppi for most of the yarns and it put a little space between weft picks, so I didn't alternate it with the warp yarn this time. Since my thicker warp was going to create a heavier fabric, I chose to skip the ruching at the shoulder and went with a narrower warp width of 10-1/2" with the same 44" weaving length as the previous cowls. Remember to vary the width of your weft stripes for interest (see proportion p. 23). Symmetry is not your friend here. Your stash buster will be more interesting with variety instead.

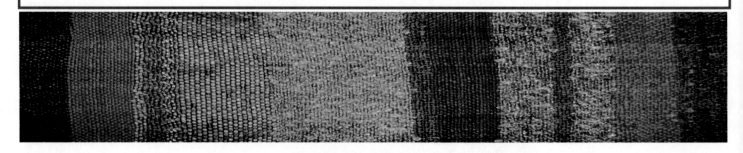

WHIP
UP A
BAG!

This useful tote has 6 outside pockets and a roomy, lined interior. It comes together in no time, sewing with cotton canvas fabric to sport a woven swatch and strap of handspun or other wooly textures.

Degree of Difficulty: Intermediate

Details on this challenge: Use your sewing skills to display quick pieces made with special yarns. The strap shown is worked on an Inkle loom (if you have one and know how to use it), or you can create it on your rigid heddle loom. The bag front, woven swatch incorporates leno, warp floats, and brooks bouquet. You can find instruction on these on p. 13.

Approx. Finished Dimensions: Bag Body will be about 16-3/4" W x 9-3/4" H x 4-1/2" D. The swatch piece for the front will be approximately 7-1/2" W x 8-1/2" L before applied to the bag.

Equipment

Rigid heddle loom with a minimum 10" weaving width

5 dent reed

1 Stick shuttle

10" min. width pick-up stick

Sewing machine (will need to handle multiple thicknesses well), thread, pins and tapestry needle

Steam iron

A straight edge ruler and pen to mark and cut fabric pieces squarely

Inkle loom (optional)

A = [5 BULKY]

B = [6 SUPER BULKY]

or [5 BULKY]

Materials

A = 120 yards bulky handspun for swatch piece and braids (or other thick and thin, bulky gauge yarn like Malabrigo Rasta or Caracol). Variegated and textured yarns add interest. Additional yarn for the strap noted below.

B= (for bag strap worked on an **inkle loom**) 1 skein Hikoo Super-Quick Alpaca #1034, 55 yds. (uses 39 yds.) and handspun (A), 17 yards. You can use A for the entire strap if desired (66 yards needed).

If weaving the strap on your rigid heddle loom you will need about 45 yards of A in addition to the swatch yarn needed.

3/4 yard each of: cotton duck canvas and a light weight coordinating fabric for lining (min. 44/45 width).

1/2 yard Pellon 809 Décor-Bond iron-on backing 45" W.

Large button for Closure.

Yarn Advice

Make sure your yarn is strong enough to be used as warp and that the yarn will fit comfortably into the holes of the 5 dent reed. You will use the same yarn for warp and weft in the swatch.

Warp Swatch 10" wide x 34" long (50 ends)

Weave Swatch

Weave as shown in the chart at right, completing each weave in order from top to bottom. See p. 12 for instructions on these. I've noted inches, reps (repeats), and # of picks as applicable. **At the same time,** after the first 1-1/2 of plain weave, complete a hem stitch on the beginning edge. Finish with plain weave until the piece measures 10" under tension, then hemstitch at the ending edge. YouTube has several videos for hemstitching on the rigid heddle if needed. Alternatively, you can double zigzag to raw finish the ends (p. 15) on your machine as they will be hidden in the pocket seams.

When finished, remove from the loom. Trim any hanging tails flush and trim the fringe to within 1/2" of hemstitching or close to stitching if machine stitched. Washing is optional for this piece.

Plain Weave	Leno	Weft Floats	Brooks Bouquet
1-1/2"			
		3 reps	
2 picks			
	1 rep		
1-1/2"			
			1 rep
1-1/2"			
	1 rep		
2 picks			
		3 reps	
1-1/2"*			

*Adjust this measurement to more or less to finish the piece at 10" total.

To Weave the Strap

...on an inkle loom:

Wind 5 feet of warp onto the loom alternating 2 strands of handspun with 2 strands of Hikoo 4 times and end with 2 strands of handspun. (18 ends). If using just one yarn choice in a bulky gauge, wind 24 warp ends. The Hikoo is a super bulky, so you'll wind less with that. Weave 40" with Hikoo or alternate choice.

Cut from the loom and weave the warp ends into the fabric to clean finish the ends. The bulk of this strap will probably not allow machine stitching to raw finish ends.

...on a rigid heddle loom:

This is woven with A throughout. Warp 3" wide x 64" long. Weave 40" in plain weave. End with a footer (scrap yarn woven at the end for about 1/2").

Cut from the loom and zigzag stitch both ends 3 times over to secure. Trim close to stitching.

Construct the Bag

Cut 3 rectangular pieces from the cotton duck and from the lining fabric: one at 18" x 26" and two at 18" x 8-1/2". Below is a suggested layout on a single layer of fabric.

Measure and cut carefully for best results. I use a straight edge ruler and draw lines on the wrong side of the fabric with a pen to get good rectangles.

Cut a rectangle from the Pellon 18" x 25".

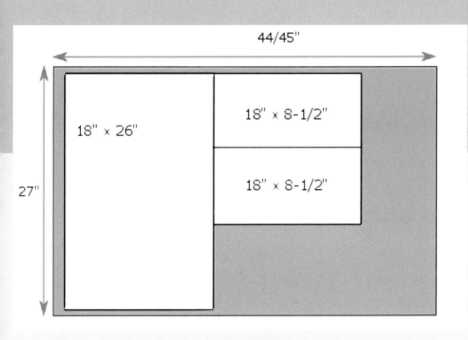

Note - Seam allowances are 1/2" throughout.

Pockets

Center and pin the swatch to the right side of the front pocket piece (fig.1). Sew along the top and bottom of the swatch as shown, about 3/8" below the edges. The fringe of your swatch may hang over the edge.

On the front of the swatch, center the button 1-1/2" below the top edge, and hand stitch in place.

Pin the right side of the pocket piece to the right side of the lining and sew along the long edges at top and bottom through all thicknesses with 1/2" seam allowance (fig. 2).

Reach into a side opening and turn the pocket piece and lining right sides out. Press at the top and bottom edges, then topstitch on the lining side along the long ends 1/4" from the edge through all thicknesses. Line the back pocket piece as you did for the front, turn that piece right sides out, and topstitch.

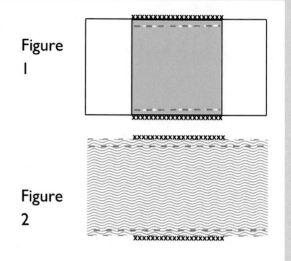

Figure 1

Figure 2

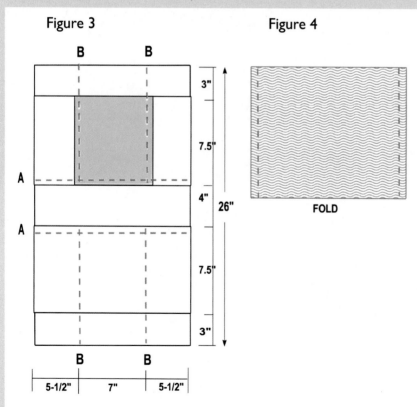

Figure 3

Figure 4

B   B

3"

7.5"

A

4"   26"

A

FOLD

7.5"

3"

B   B

5-1/2"   7"   5-1/2"

Bag Body

Reinforce the bag body by placing the rough side of the Pellon liner face down onto the wrong side of the bag body and pin together. The Pellon will be 1/2" short at each of the 18" edges. Follow the directions given with the Pellon to fuse. I like to remove the pins as I iron to keep them from getting pressed, creating dents in the fabric.

Pin the lined side of the front and back pockets to the right side of the bag body 3" from each of the 18" edges. Sew along the A and B lines (fig. 3).

Note - measurements are given to assist with placement and are approximate. Your measurements may vary slightly.

Next, fold the bag body in half with right sides together, and sew the side seams (fig. 4).

Make a Square Base

With the bag still wrong side out, take one of the bottom corners and reposition it so that it resembles figure 5 below with the side seam running up the middle and the corner flattened into a triangle. It helps to push the seam allowance in opposite directions on the front and back of this triangle. Sew as shown in step 2 below and trim the seam allowance to 1/2". Repeat at the other bottom corner. **Leave the bag body wrong side out.**

Figure 5

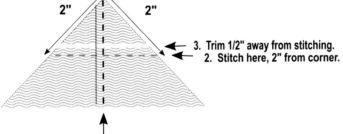

2"   2"

3. Trim 1/2" away from stitching.
2. Stitch here, 2" from corner.

1. Reposition and fold the corners of base so side seam runs exactly up the middle to a point. Fold seam allowance to the side.

Assemble and Attach the Lining

Fold the lining piece in half with right sides together and sew the side seams as in figure 4. Make a square base in the lining just as you did for the bag body (fig. 5).

Turn the lining right side out. Place the lining inside the bag body so the right sides of both are together. Pin the upper edges together, matching the side seams and easing to fit. On the back side of the bag mark 3" inward from each side seam with pins. The space between the pins reserves a 10-1/2-11" opening for pulling the bag and lining through after sewing. You need a generous gap here due to the stiffener added. Sew 1/2" from the upper edge from the first pin around the front of the bag to the 2nd pin.

Pull the liner through the gap to bring the right side out, then follow that by pulling the bag body right side out. Tuck the liner down into the bag and press around the top edge folding and pressing a hem along the edges in the liner and bag where the gap is. Sew about 3/16" from the top edge, all the way around, to seal.

...and the Finishing Touches

Braids

Option 1: Cut 18 strands of A, 28" long, to make 3 braids. Tie 6 strands together around your warping peg or the front beam of your loom to anchor them and use double strands to 3-strand braid them to the end. Tie an overhand knot at the end. Remove the other end from the peg or beam and secure it with an overhand knot. You want to wind up with a braid that is about 16" long. Repeat for the other 2 braids.

Option 2: I used 1 strand of Hikoo and 2 strands of handspun for each of the braids shown here.

Bag Closure

Fold one of the braids in half, pin it to the center back of the bag about one inch below the edge. Adjust the placement so it coordinates with the button on the front. Sew this loop to the bag wall. If your machine can handle it, hold the tie firmly in place as you sew and backstitch over the strands, just above the knots. If not, sew securely by hand.

Attach Side Straps

With the remaining 2 braids, fold them in half and tie together with an overhand knot about 1-1/2" above the end knots to make a loop. Fold each end of the bag strap around the center of these loops and stitch the strap ends closed by hand. Make sure the wrong sides are turned the same way on both ends as you sew.

Stuff one end knot of the loop into each pocket at the side seam. Double check to make sure that you've placed the wrong side of the strap inward at each side and machine stitch in place just above the knots along the pocket stitching. Repeat on the other side to finish the strap.

This is a great tote for your weaving supplies when you're on the go!

PLAY
WITH
COLOR!

This scarf was created to sample warp and weft choices for the top patterns starting on page 78. Maybe you'll want to make it to coordinate with one of those pieces?

It's one of my favorite scarves to wear due to the range of color and soft textures.

Degree of Difficulty: Easy

Details on this challenge: A scarf is a great way to sample color blends before you commit to a garment. This one specifies many colors because I planned to use the left overs elsewhere. If you are hoping to economize, you can choose to make this scarf with 2 rather than 3 color changes of A, just 1 color of B, and 1 color of C. Otherwise, leftovers can be used to create one of the tops on p. 78-79.

There are just a few tips for success when you vary the gauge and elasticity of your novelty textures in the warp. These are given in the yarn advice on the next page.

10 epi, 12 ppi
Approximate Finished Dimensions: 10" W x 65" L

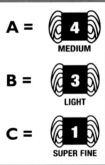

A = 4 MEDIUM

B = 3 LIGHT

C = 1 SUPER FINE

Equipment
Loom with minimum 13" weaving width

10 dent reed

2 shuttles

Materials (see Yarn Advice p. 56 for further yarn selection info.)
A = 1 skein each of Prism Kiwi, 53% cotton, 29% nylon, 18% rayon, in Blue Lagoon, Embers, and
Ginger, 2 oz = 93 yards (uses 32 yards each for the 2 colors on the perimeter and 44 yards of the color in the middle).

B = 1 skein each of Prism Tencel Tape, 100% Tencel, in Mist, Loam, and Embers (uses 16 yards each for outside colors, 22 yards in the middle).

C = 1 skein each, Mary Gavan Yarns, Desert, 50% organic cotton, 50% bamboo in Tapestry (uses 194 yards) and Sedona Sunset (uses 226 yards), 4oz = 475 yards.

Yarn Advice

Part of the appeal of this piece is the soft and fuzzy texture of the Kiwi yarn contrasted with the smooth tape yarn, Tencel Tape. If you can't locate Kiwi, a fuzzy or chenille substitute in Dk to worsted gauge will work nicely. Make sure a substitute passes the test for warp strength. Some chenille can be fragile.

Different gauge yarns placed in the same reed together will have a different take-up when woven. Puckering of the fabric along the length can be the result. if Alternating the different weights loop by loop when direct warping isolates them and keeps one from dominating the other - no puckering.

I'm breaking my rule here by adding yarns of varied elasticity. The C yarn has very little give, while the rest of the yarns are quite stretchy. The A and B ends will be shorter than the C warp ends when these yarns are wound on. You can trim the longer ends when tying onto the front as I've allowed extra warp to accommodate.

C can be carried across when direct warping without cutting and tying until the end. A can be carried for its first 2 loops in each repeat. You should cut and retie it for each repeat. B should be tied on, then cut and tied off each time it appears. Always tie to the apron rod (not yarn to yarn). Allowing alternating yarns to travel past no more than 1 loop prevents excess crossing that can restrict the opening of the shed while weaving. Firm tension and a warp stick or empty shuttle placed in the back shed opening behind the reed will also help with a clean shed. Push the stick to the back beam to keep it out of the way. This extra care is especially helpful when using yarns of varied elasticity.

Warp

Warp 12-1/4″ wide x 96″ long (122 ends) according to the chart below. See p. 12 if you need chart reading help. I found it easier to draw all of the C loops first leaving every other slot for the others. Then I went back and filled in the A and B loops.

10x						
			2		2	A
2		2				B
	2		2		2	C

In the scarf seen here, I changed the color combination after the repeats as follows:

Reps 1-3: A in Embers, B in Loam, and C in Sedona Sunset.

Reps 4-7: A in Blue Lagoon, B in Indigo, and C in Tapestry.

Reps 8-10: A in Ginger, B in Mist, and C in Sedona Sunset

The scarf shown on p. 86 is an example of making 2 rather than 3 color changes with this pattern.

Weave with C in plain weave for 78″. I changed From Sedona Sunset to Tapestry after 39″ of weaving to experiment, but this will be just as beautiful in one color for C. You can see the value change in the photo at the top of the preceding page.

Finish

Remove from the loom, tying 3 strand fringe with overhand knots.

Hand wash with mild detergent in room temperature water and hang dry. Trim ends flush and cut the fringe to the desired length.

VARY WEFT
FLOATS FOR
A CONTRAST
OF
TEXTURES!

When I put this one together, I was thinking about a nontraditional way to assemble a traditional shawl. I decided to join the pieces in the front and back in a random overlap fashion, rather than attaching it at the edge, and yet, the warp floats happen to line up across the front. I've sewn in a couple darts to enhance the fit around the shoulders.

Degree of Difficulty: Easy

Details on this challenge: We'll set our pick-up stick for a variation on a 10-step weft float. The number of repeats will be different on the 2 pieces in this garment to make them land evenly on the front overlap.

10 epi, 8 ppi for plain weave and 10 ppi for weft float pattern

Approximate Finished Dimensions (each piece, make 2): 11" W x 32" L for size Regular and 12" W x 33" L for size XLarge (bust size 46" or greater).

Change for size XL is given in parenthesis

Equipment

Loom with minimum 15" weaving width

Sewing machine, thread, pins

10 dent reed

1 shuttle

1-15" pick-up stick

10 - 11 warp sticks to weave between the 2 pieces to reserve fringe

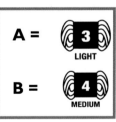

A = 3 LIGHT

B = 4 MEDIUM

Materials

A = 3 balls Schoppel Edition 3, 100% extra fine, superwash merino in #2301, 50 gm=164 yards [uses 401 (438)].

B = 4 skeins Berroco Glace, 100% rayon tape in Sage, 50 gm = 75 yards [uses 232 (249) yards].

Yarn Advice

The weft yarn chosen is a rayon tape. You can choose any worsted, solid color yarn for this, but the flat tape does help emphasize the floats in the pattern. Some weavers bother with trying to keep the ribbon flat, but I really don't see a noticeable difference if you just relax and weave. The ribbon tends to flatten out in the work and in the wash quite naturally.

Warp using A

Regular 13-1/2" wide (136 ends) x 106" long.

XLarge 14-1/2" wide (146 ends) x 108" long.

Weft Float Pattern

Set the pick-up stick by placing the heddle in the down position which leaves the slot threads as the top row.

On the warp ends of this upper row, starting on either side behind the reed, use the beveled edge of your stick to *pick up and place 3 slot ends on top of the stick, skip over 2. Repeat from * across. End with 3 ends on top of the stick. Push the stick to the back beam to be out of the way when not in use.

It is assumed, and not stated, that you will throw your shuttle through at each step below.

Pick 1. Heddle Up

Pick 2. Pick-Up (Put heddle in neutral, pull pick-up stick forward and set it upright close to the back of the reed.)

Pick 3. Heddle Up

Pick 4. Pick-Up

Pick 5. Heddle Up

Pick 6. Pick-Up

Pick 7-10. Weave plain weave

Weave with B throughout. You will make 2 pieces on one warp as follows:

Piece #1: Weave 4 picks of plain weave, then begin the 10-step, weft float pattern. Repeat the pattern 14 (15) times, then weave plain until the work measures 36 (37)".

Before you begin piece #2, weave warp sticks into alternating sheds to reserve approximately 11" for fringe in between.

Piece #2: Weave 4 picks of plain weave, then begin the 10-step, weft float pattern. Repeat the pattern 7 (8) times, then weave plain until work measures 36 (37)".

Finish Pieces

Remove the work from the loom, tying 3 strand fringe with overhand knots on each end. Cut the warp reserved for fringe between the pieces, leaving approximately 5-1/2" fringe each side, remove the warp sticks, and tie fringe tassels on these ends as well.

Hand wash with mild detergent in room temperature water and hang dry. Trim hanging tails flush and cut fringe to 4" length.

Create Darts for better fit around the neck.

The piece with the 14 (15) pattern repeats will be your right shoulder. On the wrong side of this piece (wrong side of patterned area facing you), use a straight pin to mark the dart fold 9" above the point where the pattern ends (at left selvage). Fold at the pin with the right sides together. Mark the ending point of the dart at 3 (4)" inward with a pin. Sew through both thicknesses starting at the selvage, 3/4" below the fold, and tapering the stitch line to the dart end point pin as shown below.

Create the dart for the piece with the 7 (8) pattern repeats as given above (fold line at 9" above the pattern end), but mark that fold line at the right selvage. The seam of the dart will then be approximately 8-1/4" above the patterned area. See diagram p. 62 to confirm placement.

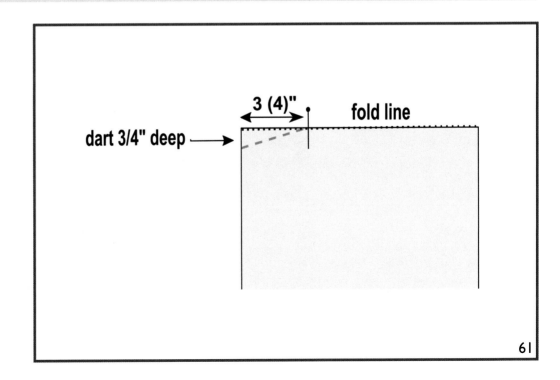

dart 3/4" deep →   3 (4)"   fold line

Assemble

Overlap the patterned ends of each piece. The end with 7 (8) repeats will be on top and should overlap by approximately 4" as shown on the diagram at right.

Level up the weft float pattern edges on the front (see diagram at right). Pin carefully and sew around 3 sides through both pieces to secure the fronts as shown.

Repeat for the back ends, overlapping the right end facing you over the left as on the front.

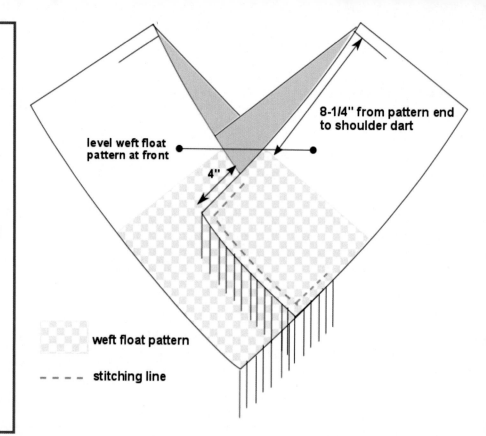

8-1/4" from pattern end to shoulder dart

level weft float pattern at front

4"

weft float pattern

- - - - stitching line

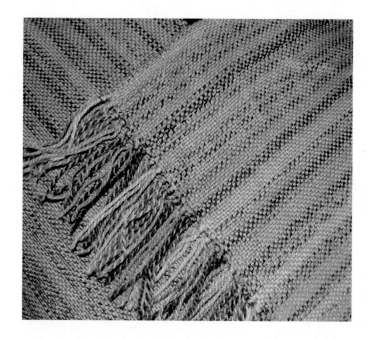

To Wear

Toss over your shoulders with the weft float pattern in the front or drape it around your neck for the cowl effect in the photo here.

GET
COZY
WITH A
BULKY
YARN!

The simple structure of this shoulder cozy requires a little basic knit and purl for fit around the shoulders. Sizes are based upon the measurement from shoulder edge to shoulder edge across the back (cross back measurement).

Degree of Difficulty: Easy

Details on this challenge: We'll use a bulky yarn closely set on an 8 dent reed for warmth, but give it some drape by alternating with a dk gauge yarn to loosen the fabric for softness and definition.

8epi, 7ppi. Knitting Gauge: approx. 10 sts and 13 rows in stockinette stitch = 4"

Sizes	Small	Medium	Large	XLarge+
Cross Back Measurement	14-1/2" - 15"	15-1/2" -16"	16-1/2" -17"	17-1/2"-18"
Yards used, A	291	303	334	343
Yards used, B	203	211	221	229

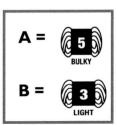

Cross back is between outside edges of shoulder bones.

Equipment

Loom with minimum 15" weaving width

8 dent reed

2 shuttles

US 15, 24" and 32" circular needles

1 large stitch marker

Large crochet hook to pick up stitches (M/N 13 or N/P 15) (a no handle hook works best)

Sewing machine, thread, pins, and tapestry needle

Materials

A = 4 balls Berroco Millefiori BIG, 50% wool, 50% acrylic in Viola, 110 gm = 93 yards.

B = 1 ball Berroco Summer Silk, 45% silk, 43% cotton, 12% nylon in Pier, 50 gm = 240 yards.

A = 5 BULKY

B = 3 LIGHT

Yarn Advice

Watch while you draw alternating loops of the 2 warp yarns to keep your pattern orderly. It's easy to snooze on the job and create a flaw in the warp...or you can refer to this as an intentional design element if you don't catch yourself!

Also, soft and wooly yarns, like Millefiori, want to stick together as they pass in the weaving, so your best choice for alternating between the loops of this yarn will be a smooth cotton blend, rayon, or silk fiber as I've chosen here rather than an animal fiber. Regardless, the soft spun texture of the bulky will make it want to bond to itself to some degree, so alternate the weft picks mindfully as you weave. Mistakes, followed by unweaving, can be a hassle with this yarn.

When starting or ending weft, tuck the tails into the same shed after you wrap the tail around the outermost warp end. For thick yarn and when alternating yarns, this will show less than tucking it into the next shed. You can also unply and remove some of the thickness of the bulky yarn for a few inches at the ends and overlap these reduced starting and ending pieces, but I find that more bother than needed on this piece.

Warp 14-3/4" wide x 82 (85, 89, 92)" long. You will alternate one loop of A,, then one loop of B across. End with one loop of A to total 14-3/4" wide (118 ends).

Weave in plain weave alternating one pick of A with one pick of B to 58 (61, 65, 68)" long.

Finish

Remove the work from the loom, tying fringe with overhand knots on both ends. Wash with mild detergent in room temperature water and hang dry. Trim hanging tails flush and cut fringe to 6" length.

Changes for sizes are given in parenthesis.

Assemble

Fold the woven piece in half with wrong sides together, fringe ends matching, as shown below. Sew through both thicknesses from the top edge (dotted red line) for just 1-1/2" at 21 (22-1/2, 23, 25-1/2)" from the fold line. Backstitch this entire seam to secure.

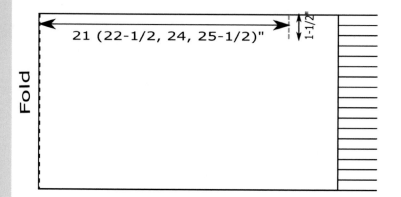

Knitted Shoulders

With the crochet hook, right side facing and starting at the seam, pick up 88 (92, 96, 100) stitches, 2 ends below the selvage and place them onto the 32" circular needles. I like to pick up several stitches with the hook, then slide them off the other end of the hook onto the knitting needles (works if you have no extra handle on your hook).

Working in the round, place a marker for the beginning of the round, P1 *K2, P2. Repeat from * to the last 3 stitches before the marker, K2, P1. Repeat for 6 more rounds,

With the 24" circular needles, complete a decrease round: P1, *K2tog, P2. Repeat from * to the last 3 stitches before the marker, K2tog, P1.

For the last 5 rounds: P1, *K1, P2, repeat from * to the last 2 stitches before the marker, K1, P1. Bind off and weave in tails.

MAKE IT
DRAPE
AND
SHAPE!

Take 100% rayon yarn, add a little chenille texture, and you have one super soft and wearable sweatshirt. We'll double the dk rayon in the body to keep up with the bulky chenille. This adds weight to the garment but lends to the drape. This piece is designed to be oversize in width and hits at high hip for length.

Degree of Difficulty: Intermediate

This pattern will walk you through how to shape a notch as you weave for the neck opening. We'll use this method with a different finish in the tops on p. 78 - 79. You'll also execute a method for double warping select ends. Finish details will include a casing formed from seam binding for an easy drawstring bottom. For non-crocheters, instructions are given for finishing the neckline with seam binding on p. 76.

Front and Back pieces: 5 epi, 10 ppi. Sleeves: 10 epi, 10 ppi

Sizes	Small	Med	Large	XLarge	2x	3x
Bust Measurement	32"-34"	36"-38"	40"-42"	44"-46"	48"-50"	52"-54"

Additional finished measurements on p. 77. Adjust for desired fit.

Yards used, A	930	942	1048	1155	1275	1358
Yards used, B	79	86	96	104	113	120

Equipment
Loom with minimum 15 (15, 18, 18, 18, 20)" weaving width

5 and 10 dent reeds

2 shuttles

Steam Iron, sewing machine, thread, pins, and tapestry needle

US H/8 Crochet hook for neckline trim. Can use 3/4 yd. additional seam binding and sew instead,.

# Materials
A = 2 (2, 3, 3, 3, 3) skeins Interlacements Zig Zag, 100% rayon in Tapestry, 4oz=500 yards.

B = 1 (1, 1, 1, 2, 2) skeins Prism Yarns, Big Chenille Layers. 100% rayon in Hibiscus, 8oz. = 111yards. 2x and 3x sizes can probably get away with 1 skein if you use an alternate yarn for the bottom tie.

Two 1/2" or wider beads with 1/4" holes to trim drawstring.

Approx. 2 feet of 1/4" wide elastic and medium safety pin to thread it.

Scrap yarn of dk gauge for header and notch weaving.

Two 3 yard packages, double fold, bias seam binding.

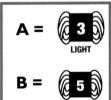

A = 3 LIGHT

B = 5 BULKY

Yarn Advice

The best results will be obtained with a yarn that is primarily rayon, bamboo, or Tencel for that "slouchy" effect.

You will be warping with double strands of A alternating with single strands of B in the garment body. Single strands of A will be used in the warp of the contrasting sleeves. When you draw the loops to double warp A in the body, note that you pull one loop through a slot and one through a hole on the chart. You won't have to sley the holes with this yarn thereafter. You'll only need to sley the empty hole that you skipped with B.

Changes for sizes are given in parenthesis.

Warp Front/Back Pieces (5 dent reed)

(according to the chart below) 12-1/2 (13-1/2, 14-3/4, 16, 17-1/4, 18-1/2)" wide. This is 62 (68, 74, 80, 86, 92) ends where double strands of A count as one. Warp length will be 118 (120, 124, 126, 128, 128)".

Using B and A according to the warp order chart below, start at the right and work to the left as you draw your loops. This chart is a representation of the slots of your reed (shaded) and heddles with holes (marked with 0). The purple stroke is a loop of B passing through a slot. Proceeding left, you skip a hole as shown, then pull a loop of A (black stroke) through a slot, the next loop of A through a hole, repeat that last pair, and end with a loop of B through a slot. Leave an empty hole last. Repeat the sequence that you completed (outlined in bold, under the green heading) for a total of 10 (11, 12, 13, 14, 15) times across.

You will need to tie on the B loop, then cut and tie it off to the apron rod each time it occurs. You can carry the A across without cutting until you are done with it because it never crosses more than 1 contrasting loop.

Once you have drawn the loops, wind on, turn the loom around to face the front and sley one of the two strands from each B loop into the adjacent empty hole to the right. You are ready to tie on to the front. A's remain double strand in their slots and holes. B's will be singles.

Warp Order:

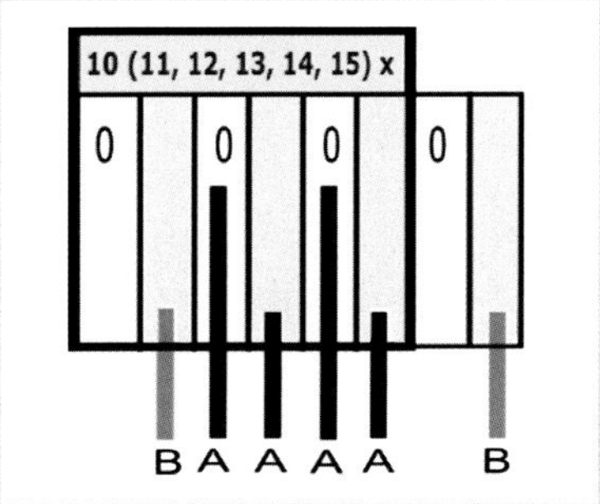

71

Weave Front/Back Pieces (make2) in plain
weave with A, using a single strand throughout, according to the weaving lengths in diagram at right, 22-1/2 (23, 24, 24-1/2, 25, 25)".

Weave the notch for the neck opening shown in
the diagram using a scrap yarn filler. See photos of this process in another pattern on p. 82-83.

To do this, throw your shuttle with A from the right, but bring it upwards, out of the shed at a point that is 6 (6, 6, 6-1/2, 6-1/2, 6-1/2)" from the left selvage, measured at the reed.

Rest this shuttle. Load your 2nd shuttle or a bobbin with scrap yarn and throw it in the same shed from the point where the first shuttle ends, leaving a short tail. You won't need to tuck this tail as you will cut away the scrap weaving later. Change your shed and throw the scrap yarn shuttle into the shed from the left to exit the front at its starting point. Pick up the shuttle with A and throw that from its ending point through the same shed to the right.

You will weave first one shuttle into a shed then the other into the same shed, side by side with no overlap for 2".

End the notch by cutting the scrap yarn and continue
weaving all the way across again with A for another 22-1/2 (23, 24, 24-1/2, 25, 25)". Weaving a straight pin into the abutting edges of the garment and the scrap yarn edges will keep a gap from forming as you continue, see photo, p. 83. You can remove the pin after you have woven about 1/2".

When the first piece is finished, cut and tuck the ending tail, weave 2 picks of scrap yarn, and weave the 2nd piece exactly as you did the first.

Finish

When complete, weave a 1/2" footer of scrap yarn (just like a header, but at the end of the work) to protect the ending edge from unraveling prior to finishing.

Weaving Measurements,

(each piece, make 2 on 1 warp)

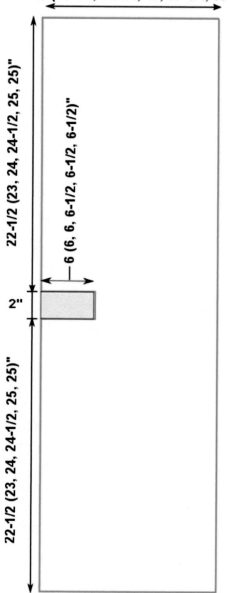

Sm   Med   Lg   XL   2X   3X
12-1/2 (13-1/2, 14-3/4, 16, 17-1/4, 18-1/2)"

22-1/2 (23, 24, 24-1/2, 25, 25)"

6 (6, 6, 6-1/2, 6-1/2, 6-1/2)"

2"

22-1/2 (23, 24, 24-1/2, 25, 25)"

Raw Finish the Ends and Neck Opening Edges

Cut the work from the loom. Double zigzag stich along the beginning and ending edges of each piece before cutting the pieces apart and trimming away the scrap yarn (see raw finish, p. 15).

Next, double zigzag the edges of the notch at each edge of the neck opening to fuse picks 2 and 3 from the edge where you wove the scrap yarn. Extend your stitching just a little beyond the inner edge of the notch to make sure no cut warp ends escape your stitching later. Cut the scrap weaving away from the stitching along that first pick at each edge.

Warp Sleeves (10 dent reed) with A, single strand, 15 (15, 15-1/2, 15-1/2, 16, 16)" wide. This is 148 (148, 154, 154, 160, 160) ends. Warp length will be 54 (56, 58, 61, 65, 68)" long.

Weave Sleeves (make 2) in plain weave with A, single strand throughout, for 15 (16, 17, 18-1/2, 20-1/2, 22)". Weave 2 picks of scrap yarn and weave the 2nd piece of equal length.

Finish

End with a 1/2" footer of scrap yarn, cut from the loom, and raw finish the edges with a double zigzag, p. 15. Wash all pieces in room temperature water with mild detergent. Hang dry and trim hanging tails flush.

Prepare seam binding to make a bottom casing and neckline reinforcements by cutting 2 pieces 46 (50, 54, 58, 62, 66)" long and 2 pieces 13" long.

If you plan to finish the neckline with binding rather than crochet, don't cut the 12" reinforcements pieces. Do cut a trim piece 30 (30, 30, 32, 32, 32)" long.

Machine wash and dry the binding pieces to make them more pliable. I've allowed for their 6% shrinkage in length and a little extra for easement.

Assemble

Center Seam:

Pin the front/back pieces (right sides) together, matching the notches for the neck opening (see drawing at right). Sew the long edge (back side) together with a "skinny seam" by stitching between the 1st and 2nd warp end of B at the edge. Sew the short edge (front) with a skinny seam also. Lightly press the seams open.

Side Seams:

Fold in half at the shoulders, right sides together. Sew underarm seams with a 1/4" seam allowance on each side

leaving 6-1/2 (7, 7-1/2, 8, 9, 9-3/4)" from the shoulder fold open for sleeves.

Sew Sleeves:

Fold the sleeve pieces in half, right sides together, matching the raw finish edges and pin. Check to make sure sleeves fit reasonably well into the armhole opening with just a little easing. If not, adjust the opening or the sleeve seam allowance. Sew a 1/4" (or adjusted) seam allowance along the raw finish edges. Press the seams open.

Fold and press a 5/8" hem to the wrong side along one selvage end of the sleeve pieces for the elastic casing. Sew this casing shut, close to the selvage, leaving a 1" wide opening for inserting elastic.

Measure loosely around your lower arm about 2/3 of the way up from your wrist to your elbow. Cut 2 pieces of elastic to this measurement plus 1/2". With a safety pin attached, thread the elastic into the casing. Making sure you don't twist it, sew the elastic together using a 1/4" seam allowance. Sew the opening in the casing closed once you test the feel around your arm. Repeat for the other sleeve.

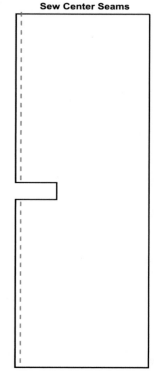

Sew Center Seams

Turn the sleeves right side out and the front/back (body) wrong side out. Inset the sleeve into the armhole opening so right sides of the fabric are together and underarm seams of the sleeve meet the underarm seams of the body.

Pin, easing to fit, and sew around the sleeve edge through both thicknesses with a 1/4" seam allowance. Repeat for the other sleeve. Turn front/back right side out and press the seam flat.

Bottom (outside) Casing:

Open both of the long pieces of binding at the center fold and press it flat so it is 1" wide with folded edges. On one piece, open both edge folds (drawing at right). Turn a 5/8" hem on one end, press, and stitch close to the fold.

With one edge fold of the binding open, place the binding along the bottom of the garment (right sides together). See the drawing below. Position the hemmed end of the binding at the center front seam.

Pin the binding around the bottom raw edge. At the end of the round, fold a hem in the binding so it meets the other hemmed end at the center front seam. While the rest of the binding to this point is still pinned in place, carefully fold, press, and sew the hem at this loose end as for the beginning. Cut this folded hem allowance to 5/8". This will create a finished opening at the front to pull out ties as detailed in the top photo on p. 76.

Pin the ending edge just hemmed in place and sew the binding to the front/back bottom edge all the way around. Leave this binding piece as is until you have attached the bottom (inside) casing as instructed on the next page.

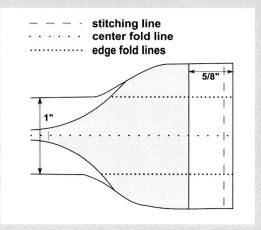

- – – – · stitching line
- · · · · · · center fold line
- ············ edge fold lines

1"

5/8"

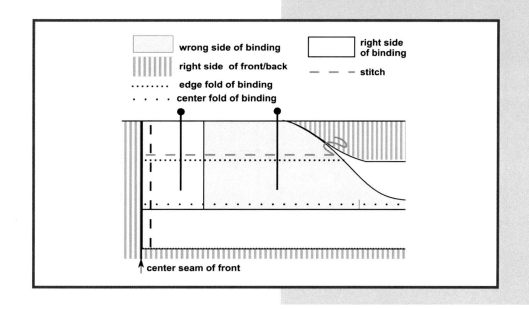

wrong side of binding

right side of binding

right side of front/back

– – – stitch

········ edge fold of binding

· · · · center fold of binding

↑ center seam of front

Bottom (inside) Casing: Starting at a side seam, attach the 2nd long piece of binding, opening one edge fold to pin the right side of this binding to the opposite (wrong) side of the garment around the bottom. You won't need to hem these binding ends. Simply overlap them by 5/8" and sew around, close to the edge fold.

Turn the binding on both sides of the garment down (right sides out) and press. Folded edges along the bottom of the binding pieces are now together.

To seal the casing, sew the 2 pieces of binding together around the bottom, close to the folded edges.

Make the bottom tie: Cut 3 strands of B to match the measurement around the bottom of your garment plus 20". Tie them together at one end and loop that end around your warping peg or front beam on your loom to anchor.

3-strand braid them together tightly, tie a knot at the end, then remove from the peg or beam.

Attach a large safety pin to one end of the braid and thread the tie through the bottom casing. Try on your sweatshirt to adjust the length of the ties according to your preference. I like my ties short (about 3" long before drawn). You will lose about 1" of length on each end when you add the beads and tie the knots so take that into consideration.

Slide a bead onto the braid on each end, then tie 2 knots (one over the other) to keep the bead from slipping off.

Neck Finishing with crochet: With the shorter pieces cut from the seam binding, open one edge fold and pin it along the width of the raw finished edges at the front and back neck. Sew the binding to the neck edges close to the raw edge of the fabric, then trim away the rest of this binding close to your stitching. This little piece of binding will reinforce the raw edges so you can crochet over it on these non-selvage edges.

Single crochet around the entire neck opening with a double strand of A, covering the binding reinforcement you completed at the front and back edges. Half double crochet one more round, cut the yarn, and weave in the tail.

Neck Finishing if you don't crochet: With the final piece of seam binding you cut as given on p. 74, open the center and edge folds, fold one end over 5/8" to wrong side, and press. Pin the right side of the binding to the right side of the neck edge at one shoulder seam all the way around the neck opening starting with this folded edge. When you get around to the start, overlap the folded end by 5/8" and cut the binding. Sew around the neck opening between the neck edge and the edge fold, close to the fold, easing the binding carefully to fit around the corners.

Fold the binding at the center fold so the other edge fold is pressed to the inside of the neck opening and sew through all thicknesses about 1/8" away from the folded edge., easing the binding around the corners. Take care to feel that the folded outside and inside edges of the binding line up as you sew. Press around the neckline. This is similar to the neck finish shown on the tops on p. 78 - 79, but without the front opening.

Finished Measurements after Seaming and Trim

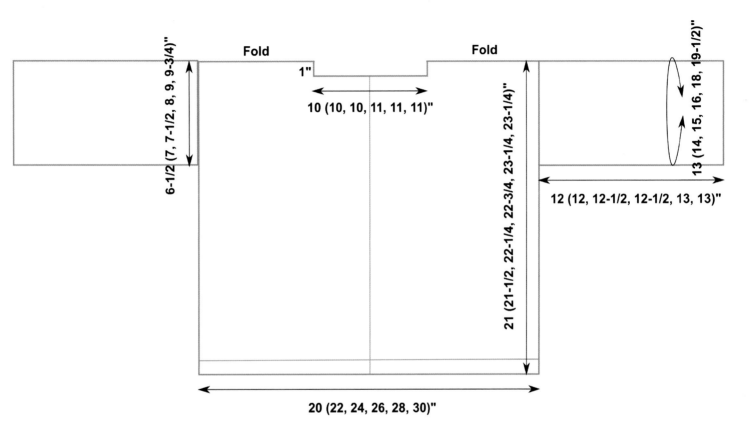

Fold   Fold

1"

6-1/2 (7, 7-1/2, 8, 9, 9-3/4)"

10 (10, 10, 11, 11, 11)"

13 (14, 15, 16, 18, 19-1/2)"

21 (21-1/2, 22-1/4, 22-3/4, 23-1/4, 23-1/4)"

12 (12, 12-1/2, 12-1/2, 13, 13)"

20 (22, 24, 26, 28, 30)"

Note – as the garment relaxes and shapes to your body, the length may expand about an inch or so from the initial finished length.

TRY VARIATIONS ON A THEME!

The sport tops on these 2 pages evolved as alternate versions of one design to attempt to make it work for a variety of tastes, skills, and body types.

At left is version 1, with knitted trim, or you can try the alternate, at right, without the knitting...

or you can just knit around the armhole (left) and finish with a round hem (right) rather than a knitted hem ...

or add your own ideas! How about a tunic length using a longer warp? Possibilities abound.

**Version 1:
With
Knitted
Trim**

Details on this challenge: To make a personalized version of this garment, take a look at the, sleeve trim, bottom border, plaid design, and fur texture added. Follow the pattern of version 1 or 2 OR choose the options that suit you best to make your own version! Note that the setup for the rounded hem of version 2 will require the longer warp given in that piece.

Skills will include notch weaving for neck shaping, plaid matching, curved hem creation, and handling varied elasticity in the warp. Knitters will get advice on how to pick up stitches along raw finish hems (non-selvage).

10 epi, 12 ppi. Knitting gauge is not significant as all knitting added in this piece will have substantial stretch.

Sizes	Small	Med	Large	XLarge	2x	3x
Bust Measurement	32"–34"	36"–38"	40"–42"	44"–46"	48"–50"	52"–54"
Yards used (A)	132	147	163	180	196	214
Yards used (B) warp	59	67	75	83	91	100
Yards used (B) knitted border	123	137	146	161	175	189
Yards used (C)	538	600	674	748	826	906
Yards used (D)	86	91	94	97	100	106

> See p. 87 for changes for Version 2, No Knitting

Equipment
Rigid heddle loom with a minimum 12 (13, 15, 15, 18, 18)" weaving width
10 dent reed
1 shuttle
Steam iron, sewing machine, thread, pins and tapestry needle
US 7, 16" (or a set of double points) and 32" circular knitting needles if adding knitted finishes around armhole and bottom.
US G6 crochet hook for picking up stitches (sharp hook head and no added handle are preferred)

A = 4 MEDIUM   C = 1 SUPER FINE
B = 3 LIGHT   D = 3 LIGHT

Materials
A = 2 (2, 2, 2, 3, 3) skeins Prism Kiwi, 53% cotton, 29% nylon, 18% rayon in Embers, 2 oz = 93 yards.
B = 2 skeins Prism Tencel Tape, 100% Tencel, 2 oz = 120 yards.
C = 2 skeins Mary Gavan Yarns Desert, 50% organic cotton, 50% bamboo in Autumn Leaves, 4oz = 475 yards.
1/2 yard double fold, bias seam binding for neck trim.
Optional for sleeves: D = 1 (1, 1, 2, 2, 2) skein Prism Plumette Layers, 100% nylon, in Bittersweet. 2 oz = 95 yards.

Yarn Advice

This is a long warp, but manageable if you roll on carefully and pack the warp well. The Kiwi and Tencel Tape have a certain amount of stretch, so I've added a couple inches to the warp length to accommodate their contraction once you remove the yarn from the peg.

Regardless, don't pull too tightly as you draw those loops. This will minimize the relative loss in length. When you tie on to the front, the C warp ends will be a few inches longer as it does not stretch like the other yarns. You can trim the extra from this yarn to make it easier to tie onto the rod as I've allowed extra length for this.

Note - make sure to use a pressing cloth and low steam setting where advised due to the nylon content in some of the yarn.

Warp (Version 1) according to the warp order

chart below. Changes for sizes are given in parenthesis. I prefer to draw all the C loops first in my direct warp, leaving spaces to go back and draw the A and B loops. A will need to be tied on, cut, and retied to the rod after the first 2 loops in each repeat. B will need to be tied on, cut and retied to the rod at each repeat. This is to avoid excess crossing of warp ends.

Warp width: 11-1/2 (12-1/2, 13-3/4, 15, 16-1/4, 17-1/2)" wide. This is 114 (126, 138, 150, 162, 174) ends. Length of warp will be 118 (120, 122, 124, 126, 128)"

Warp Order:

See p. 12 for instructions on reading warp order charts.

			9 (10, 11, 12, 13, 14)x				
2	2			2		2	A
		2					B
	2	2	2	2			C

Weave (make 2) with C in plain weave according to the

weaving measurements for your size shown in the drawing on p. 83. For each of the 2 pieces, you'll weave the longer side (the back) first, create a notch, and end that piece with the shorter side (the front).

Weave the notch for the neck opening shown in

the drawing using a scrap yarn filler as follows:

Throw your shuttle with A from the right, but bring it upwards, out of the shed at a point that is 3-1/2 (3-1/2, 3-1/2, 4, 4, 4)" from the left selvage, <u>measured at the reed</u>.

Load your 2nd shuttle or a bobbin with scrap yarn and throw it in the same shed from the point where the first shuttle ends, leaving a short tail. You won't need to tuck this tail as you will cut away the scrap weaving later. Next, change your shed and throw the scrap yarn shuttle into the shed from the left to exit the front at its starting point. Throw the shuttle with A from its ending point through the same shed all the way to the right.

You will weave first one shuttle into a shed then the other into the same shed, side by side with no overlap for 3", leaving an open slot between the garment and the scrap weaving. See the photo below.

Warp Width and Weaving Lengths, Version 1: With Knitted Trim (each piece, make 2 on 1 warp)

Sm   Med   Lg   XL 2X   3X
11-1/2 (12-1/2, 13-1/2, 15, 16, 17-1/2)"

21-1/2 (22, 22-1/2, 23, 23-1/2, 24)"

3-1/2 (3-1/2, 3-1/2, 4, 4, 4)"

scrap yarn

3" ← filler for neck

Sew Center Seams

22-1/2 (23, 23-1/2, 24, 24-1/2, 25)"

End the notch by cutting the scrap yarn. Weave all the way across again with A. Before you weave across, use a straight pin to join the selvages at the abutting edges of the garment and the scrap weaving (as shown below). This will keep the warp ends from pulling apart and creating a gap as you resume.

After you have woven about 1/2", you can remove the pin. Weave the remainder of this piece, then cut and tuck the ending tail. Weave 2 picks of scrap yarn and complete the 2nd piece exactly as you did the first.

Finish (when both pieces are complete) by weaving a 1/2" footer of scrap yarn (just like a header, but at the end of the work) to protect the ending edge prior to sewing.

Cut the work from the loom. Double zigzag stitch along the beginning and ending edges of each piece before cutting the pieces apart and trimming away the scrap yarn (see p. 15). Raw finish the notches as described on p. 73.

Hand wash both pieces in room temperature water with mild detergent. Hang dry and trim hanging tails flush.

Cut 23 (24)" of seam binding for neck opening. Wash and dry the binding piece to make it more pliable. I've allowed for the 6% shrinkage in length.

Assemble

Center Seam: Right sides together, pin front/back pieces together, matching notches for neck opening (see drawing at left). Sew the long side (back) with a "skinny seam" up to the notch by stitching 2 warp ends inward from the selvage. Sew the shorter center seam (front) with a skinny seam, <u>leaving 5-1/4" open for the front V</u>. Lightly press the seams open using a pressing cloth.

Side Seam: Fold in half at shoulders, with right sides together. Sew underarm seams with a skinny seam on each side leaving 8-1/2 (9, 9-1/4. 9-1/2, 10, 10-1/2)" from the shoulder fold open for armholes.

Finish Neck Opening

Open one edge fold of the binding. Starting at one side of the front neck opening, extend the binding 5/8" beyond the selvage and pin it to the fabric around the neck, right sides together (see diagram below). Sew between the fold and neck edge, close to the fold.

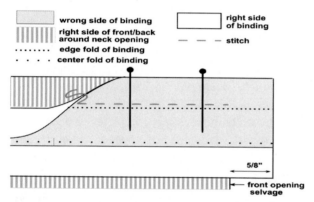

Close the edge fold and tuck extended ends of the binding inward. Fold the binding over the neck edge to encase and pin it closed.

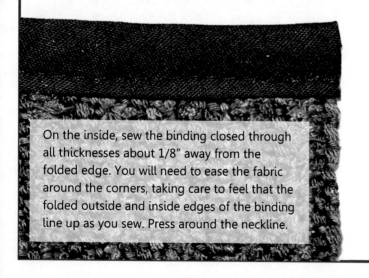

On the inside, sew the binding closed through all thicknesses about 1/8" away from the folded edge. You will need to ease the fabric around the corners, taking care to feel that the folded outside and inside edges of the binding line up as you sew. Press around the neckline.

Finished Measurements

Shown below are the finished measurements of version 1. The ribbed bottom border allows you to adjust the final length. Knitting of both the sleeves and the bottom border will draw in toward the bound off edges to hug arms and hips.

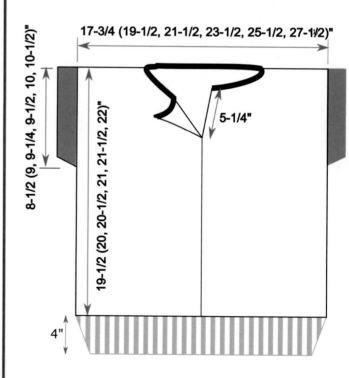

Knitted Sleeves

With the crochet hook, on the right side of the fabric, pick up 68 (72, 74, 76. 80, 84) stitches around the armhole opening, 2 ends below the selvage. Place them onto the 16" circular needle. I like to pick up several stitches with the hook, then slide them off the other end of the hook onto the knitting needles (works if you have no extra handle).

Place a marker for the start of the round. Work 25 rows of garter stitch in the round (knit 1 row, purl 1 row). The fur has no stitch definition, so it's a good idea to count your stitches frequently to make sure none were dropped and keep close track of the row count. Bind off loosely and weave in all tails.

Knitted Bottom Border

Fold a 3/8" hem around the bottom of the garment and press. Stitch 1/4" from the folded edge. While you should never pick up stitches along a raw finish edge, it works to pick them up along the fold once the hem is sewn.

With the crochet hook, right side facing you, pick up 144 (156, 172, 188, 204, 220) stitches around the bottom, 2 picks from the folded edge and place them onto the 32" circular needle. It helps if the head of your crochet hook is pointed. This makes it easier to poke into the threads at the fold. Place a marker for the start of the round. Work in K2, P2 for 34 rounds (4") or until desired length is achieved. Bind off loosely and weave in all tails.

Version 2: No Knitting

Shown with coordinating scarf. This is a 2 color scheme variation of the pattern on p. 54.

Ready for a Challenge?

This is a simple piece by construction. This pattern will require just a little extra focus as you are alternating multiple yarns of varied gauge in both warp and weft. Matching the horizontal plaid when weaving and sewing is what requires the extra care, but it can't all be easy...unless you want it to be. It's perfectly fine to ratchet down the challenge by warping according to the chart for the knitted trim version and eliminate the faux fur stripe. Then you just plain weave with the lace gauge C. If you do this, be sure you use the warp length for version 2 as the rounded hem requires a longer warp than the knitted border. You'll need about 12% more of the warp and weaving yarns remaining once you eliminate the extra striping yarns.

I've chosen colors that are somewhat monochromatic here. Try this with a little more color contrast if you like a bolder statement.

Version 2 is made with the same equipment and the same yarns (plus a couple extra). The weaving order, length, hem, and armhole finish are the key differences.

10 epi, 12 ppi,

Sizes	Small	Med	Large	XLarge	2x	3x
Bust Measurement	32"-34"	36"-38"	40"-42"	44"-46"	48"-50"	52"-54"
Yards used (A)	125	152	162	174	185	204
Yards used (B)	46	47	54	62	70	72
Yards used (C1)	405	446	499	560	611	672
Yards used (C2)	163	179	200	225	245	269
Yards used (D)	53	54	61	69	77	79
Yards used (E)	9	10	10	11	12	14

Equipment
Rigid heddle loom with a minimum 12 (13, 15, 15, 18, 18)" weaving width
10 dent reed
3 shuttles
Steam iron, sewing machine, thread, and pins

Gauges for A-D, see p. 81.

E =

Materials
A = 2 skeins Prism Kiwi, 53% cotton, 29% nylon, 18% rayon in Embers, 2 oz = 93 yards.
B = 2 (2, 2, 3, 3, 3) skeins Prism Tencel Tape, 100% Tencel, 2 oz = 120 yards.
C1 = 1 (1, 2, 2, 2, 2) skeins Mary Gavan Yarns Desert, 50% organic cotton, 50% bamboo in Autumn Leaves, 4oz = 475 yards.
C2 = 1 skein, Mary Gavan Yarns Desert in Spring Green.
D = Prism Plumette Layers 87% nylon, 13% polyester in Conifer, 2 oz = 95 yards.
E = 1 ball Vinni's Colors Serina in Black, 50 gm = 120 yards. You can use any yarn scraps of similar weight.
1/2 yard double fold, bias seam binding for neck trim.

Warp Width and Weaving Lengths, Version 2: No Knitting
(each piece, make 2 on 1 warp):

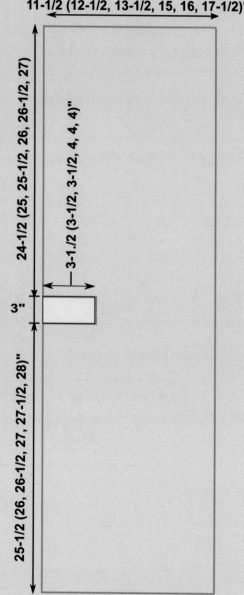

Sm   Med   Lg   XL 2X 3X
11-1/2 (12-1/2, 13-1/2, 15, 16, 17-1/2)"

24-1/2 (25, 25-1/2, 26, 26-1/2, 27)

3-1./2 (3-1/2, 3-1/2, 4, 4, 4)"

3"

25-1/2 (26, 26-1/2, 27, 27-1/2, 28)"

Warp (Version 2) according to the warp order chart

below. See p. 12 for chart reading advice if needed. Changes for sizes are given in parenthesis. The boundaries where you start and end are defined for each size under the chart.

I prefer to draw all of the C loops first in my direct warp, leaving spaces to go back and draw the A, B, and D loops. You can carry C across without cutting until the end. A will need to be tied on, cut, and retied to the rod after the first 2 loops in each repeat. B and D will need to be tied on, cut, and retied to the rod each time they appear. This is to avoid excess crossing of warp ends.

Warp width: 11-1/2 (12-1/2, 13-3/4, 15, 16-1/4, 17-1/2)" wide. This is 114 (126, 138, 150, 162, 174) ends. Length of warp will be 118 (120, 122, 124, 126, 128)"

Warp Order:

			7 (7, 8, 9, 10, 10) x									
2			2		2				2		2	A
						2						B
	2		2		2		2		2		2	C1
		2						2				D

XLarge

Small and 2x

Large

Medium and 3x

Weave for the plaid pattern according to the chart at right, repeating from top - down. This is for number of picks. Weave the length for your size according to the diagram at left following the notch weaving instructions on p. 82-83. When adding the single pick of E, tuck the tails in the same shed on both sides by wrapping them around the outermost warp end. I don't bother with a shuttle for E. I just cut and push the single pick through with my fingers.

A	C1	C2	E
	14		
		6	
2			
		6	
	14		
2			
	14		
			1

At the same time you are weaving the notch, when you get to 26-1/2 (27, 27-1/2, 28, 28-1/2, 29)" length, stop weaving, mark the place where you stopped on the chart. Weave 1 pick with E, then reverse the pattern weaving from the point marked on the chart - upward, one time through. Continue weaving the full chart bottom - up, until the first piece is complete. This will match the plaid between front and back. Weave 2 picks of scrap yarn. Repeat for the 2nd piece.

Finish and Assemble per the instructions given for version 1, p. 83 - 84 with two added considerations:

1. When pinning the center and side seams use the horizontal picks of E as your guides to match the plaid. Place a pin through both thicknesses to make E line up on the front and back before sewing the pieces together carefully. Use a long stitch in case you need to correct any spots that may be more than a little off.

2. Besides the opening for armholes along the side seams, leave a 4-1/2" opening at the bottom for side slits.

Create a rounded hem

On the front, wrong side, turn up one bottom corner so it creates a triangle with 3-1/2" sides, with the skinny side seam allowance pressed flat (fig.1 below). Next, ease the diagonal edge so that it rounds nicely and pin (fig.2). The corner fabric will pucker as a result of the rounding, but this will be cut away after sewing.

Turning a 1/2" hem across the front, repeat rounding for the other front corner, and press the entire hem using a pressing cloth. Note - your hem allowance will start out narrow at the skinny seam allowance but will get wider to 1/2" around the curve and across the bottom. It narrows again at the other side seam as it merges into the skinny seam allowance there.

Sew the hem closed with a straight stitch starting at the top of the side slit in the small seam allowance of one side. Continue sewing around the corner, across to the other corner, around,

and up to top of the other side slit seam allowance.

Next, remove the pins, turn the excess corner fabric out so you can zigzag stitch twice through the single thickness of this excess close to the stitching of the hem (running the zigzag from the selvage to the existing zigzag along the bottom edge). Repeat at the other corner and trim the extra fabric from the corners at each side, close to the zigzag stitch. Repeat for the back. Your top is ready to wear.

Fig. 3 below shows an inside corner of the completed raw finish hem after trimming. The little tufts of fiber around the curve and at bottom edge show you the texture of the faux fur and kiwi yarns up close.

Finished Measurements after Hemming

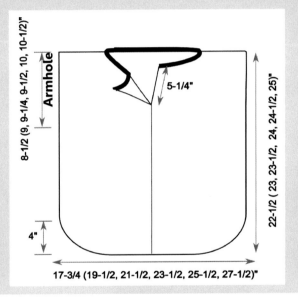

Figure 1

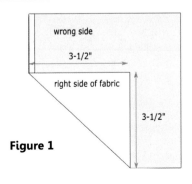

Figure 2

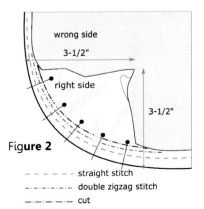

- - - - - straight stitch
-·-·-·- double zigzag stitch
-··-··- cut

Figure 3

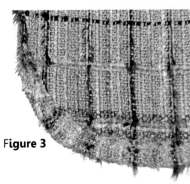

TRY A NEW TWIST ON BROOKS BOUQUET!

Create this stylish vest using a combination of worsted and sock gauge yarns with a super soft alpaca blend. Weave the front panel as a scarf only or continue onward to incorporate it into the vest shown - your choice!

Degree of Difficulty: Scarf is Easy.

Vest is Intermediate due to sewing skills required.

Details on this challenge: I stumbled across a weave online referred to as lozenge weave for the rigid heddle (origin unidentified), but I wanted to improve its symmetry, so I changed it somewhat. I'll call this one a modified lozenge weave. It's really a brooks bouquet sandwiched in plain weave.

You will warp 3 times to create all 4 pieces of the vest.

10 epi, 9 ppi for scarf front, 14 ppi for side and back panels
Front piece, scarf only, finished measurements just over 7-1/2 (7-1/2, 8, 8, 8, 8-1/2)" W x 64 (66, 68, 70, 72, 73)" L

Vest Sizes (see additional finished measurements p. 95)

	Small	Med	Large	XLarge	2x	3x
Bust Measurement	32"-34"	36"-38"	40"-42"	44"-46"	48"-50"	52"-54"
Yards used A	640	685	775	828	920	965
Yards used B	271	304	361	402	458	501

Equipment
Rigid heddle loom with a minimum 13 (15, 18, 20, 24, 24)" weaving width
8 dent reed
1 shuttle
Steam iron, sewing machine, thread, and pins
Locking stitch markers like knitters use are handy for marking placement

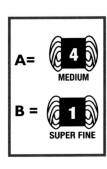

A= 4 MEDIUM

B = 1 SUPER FINE

# Materials
A = 3 (4, 4, 4, 5, 5) skeins Misti Alpaca, Tonos Worsted, 50% baby alpaca, 50% merino wool in Sahara Rust TW50, 100 gm = 218 yards.

B = 1 (1, 1, 1, 2, 2) skeins Misti Alpaca, Tonos Carnaval, 50% superfine alpaca, 30% merino, 10% silk, 10% nylon in Sahara Rust TF53, 100 gm = 436 yards.

3/4 (3/4, 1, 1, 1, 1-1/4) yard(s) double fold, bias seam binding for side panel trim.

Yarn Advice

The scarf front piece uses the worsted gauge for both warp and weft to lend body to the piece.

The remaining panels use a sock weight weft for a lighter fabric with more drape. You may want to pack the front beam with warp sticks, firm paper, or the cardboard core of a paper towel or wrapping paper roll as this lighter fabric rolls over the front knots. This will keep your fell line straighter as you weave.

If you are using this for the scarf only and want a more flexible fabric, you will use 1 (1, 2, 2, 2, 2,) skeins of worsted for warp and 1 skein of the sock weight for weft. If you prefer the worsted for the heavier weft as written for the vest, you will use an additional 1 (1, 1, 2, 2, 2) skeins of the worsted.

Alpaca has a lot of give, although the wool content of this yarn lends stability. Use tight tension and a firm beat for consistency.

Warp Scarf (front piece A) with A, 9-3/4 (9-3/4, 10-3/4, 10-3/4, 11-1/2, 11-1/2)" wide. This is 78 (78, 86, 86, 92, 92) ends. Warp length will be 93 (95, 97, 100, 102, 103)".

Weave Scarf with A in modified lozenge pattern as follows. Take the time to adjust the tension of the weft surrounding each bundle created in step 3 (after you beat that pick). The bundles at the left side of the fabric may be tighter than the ones formed at the right.

1. Starting from the right side, weave 6 picks of plain weave.

2. Insert your shuttle into the next open shed, going left under 6 (6, 5, 5, 7, 7) warp ends of the upper row and bring the shuttle up and out of the shed at that point.

3. Go back 3 warp ends of the upper row and insert the shuttle from the top, back down into the shed opening (going left) and under 9 warp ends of the upper row.

Bring the shuttle back up out of the shed at that point. This step will create bundles of warp threads that are wrapped by weft like a lasso and 6 ends that are plain weave between each bundle. The number of ends you pass under will vary at the beginning and end of the pick as noted by your size.

4. Repeat step 3 across. The last time you insert your shuttle (left edge), there will be 6 (6, 5, 5, 6, 6) warp ends remaining to pass under.

5. Weave 1 pick plain weave to return shuttle to the right.

Repeat steps 1-5 until the piece measures 69 (71, 73, 76, 78, 79)" under tension.

Finish

Remove the work from the loom, tying 3 strand fringe tassels with overhand knots on both ends. Set aside to wash with the remaining pieces.

Warp Side Panels (B), using A, 12-1/4 (14-3/4, 16-1/2, 19, 21, 23-1/2)" wide. This is 98 (118, 132, 152, 168, 188) ends. Warp length will be 61 (62, 62, 63, 63, 64, 64)".

Weave Side Panels (make 2) with B in plain weave 18-1/2 (19, 19, 19-1/2, 20, 20)". Weave 2 picks of scrap yarn and weave 2nd piece of same length.

Finish

Remove the work from the loom, tying 3 strand fringe with overhand knots on both ends. Raw finish the non-fringe ends that are separated by 2 picks of scrap yarn (see p. 15). Cut the 2 pieces apart and set aside to wash with the remaining pieces.

Warp Center Back Panel (C) using A, 8-3/4 (8-3/4, 10, 10, 11-1/4, 11-1/4)" wide. This is 70 (70, 80, 80, 90, 90) ends. Warp length will be 52 (52, 53, 53, 54, 55)".

Weave Center Back Panel (make 1) with B in plain weave 27-1/2 (28, 28-1/2, 29, 29-3/4, 30-1/2)".

Finish

Cut the work from the loom, tying 3 strand fringe with overhand knots at the ending edge. Raw finish the starting end and cut the scrap yarn away.

Hand wash all pieces in room temperature water with mild detergent. Hang dry and trim hanging tails flush. The fringe will be trimmed after the vest is assembled. Cut 2 pieces of seam binding 11 (13, 15, 17, 18, 20)" long, wash, and dry.

Assemble

For the finished measurements on p. 95, you will have used about 1/8-3/16" of fabric width for seam allowances, If your pieces are significantly different in size, the armhole area is a very general fit to accommodate differences in length. You can adjust the amount of front overlap when wearing if the end results vary in width.

Attach C to A: Decide which sides of these pieces will be the right sides. Sometimes one side looks better than the other. On the wrong side, mark the center of scarf A with a pin or locking stitch marker. Pin the right side of the back panel C (raw finish edge) to the wrong side of A, centering C around the marker. Overlap C about 3/8" over A and pin the two together at each selvage of C.

Turn the 2 pieces over, right sides facing you. Pull the center of A between the pins down 1" and round out the back neckline as shown in fig.1, opposite page. This forms a curved neckline on the back. Pin carefully around the scarf edge, remove the wrong side pins and sew the 2 pieces together close to the edge of A through both thicknesses. The wrong side will look like fig. 2 on the opposite page when sewn.

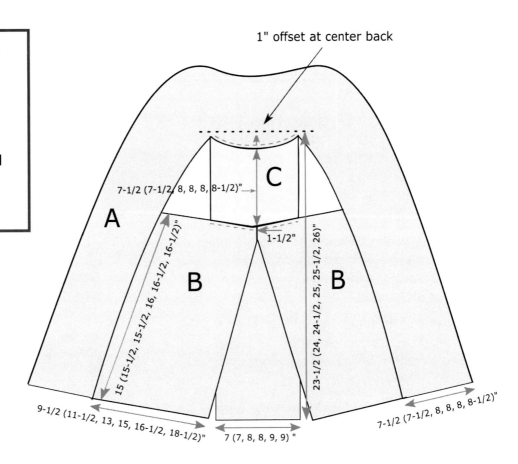

Figure 1: Finished Measurements after Seaming

Fringe across bottom edge is not shown and not included in measurements.

1" offset at center back

7-1/2 (7-1/2, 8, 8, 8-1/2)"

A

C

1-1/2"

B

15 (15-1/2, 15-1/2, 16, 16-1/2, 16-1/2)"

23-1/2 (24, 24-1/2, 25, 25-1/2, 26)"

B

9-1/2 (11-1/2, 13, 15, 16-1/2, 18-1/2)"

7 (7, 8, 8, 9, 9) "

7-1/2 (7-1/2, 8, 8, 8, 8-1/2)"

Figure 2: Neckline at Center Back

(wrong side)

95

Finish raw edge of B side panels: Press the seam binding pieces open at the center fold. To create a **folded hem with wide encased edge**, open one edge fold, pin this edge, right sides together, along the raw finish edge of a side panel matching the starting end of the tape to the selvage of the panel.

Sew close to the edge fold. Trim any excess tape at either side to line up with the selvage.

With binding edge folds closed, press the wrong side of the binding to the wrong side of fabric so that the panel measures the length from fold to fringe end shown for B in fig. 1, p. 95. I've folded about 1/2" of the woven fabric for this hem. Sew the hem close to the tape edge, fig 4. Complete for both pieces of B.

Join side panels (center back seam): With right sides together, starting at the hemmed edges, sew a skinny seam (2 ends inward from the selvage) that is 1-1/2" long. Press seam flat on the outside

Pin a side panel to the inner edge of scarf front A with right sides together, matching from the fringe edges upward. Sew together with a skinny seam and repeat for other side panel. Press seams flat.

Attach side panels to center back panel: Place the center back seam of side panels on top of the center back panel 7-1/2 (7-1/2, 8, 8, 8, 8-1/2)" below the scarf edge at center and sides. This creates a V for a slight flare at the hip (fig.5). Adjust the height here to allow the panels to hang evenly across the bottom of the vest. Pin carefully. You may want to try on your vest before you finalize this last seam to see that it hangs properly all the way around. Sew between all thicknesses 3/8 below the edge of the side panels. See stitching lines, fig. 1.

Trim fringe even around the bottom (approximately 4" long) and your vest is ready to wear.

Figure 3

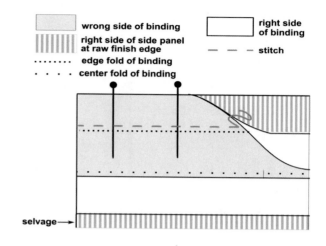

wrong side of binding

right side of side panel at raw finish edge

.... edge fold of binding

· · · · · center fold of binding

right side of binding

— — — stitch

selvage→

Figure 4

Figure 5

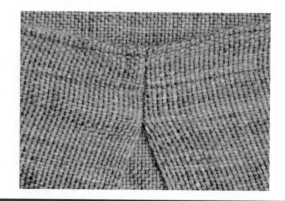

GET WILD WITH NOVELTY YARNS!

> *The textural collar in this shrug is made from a unique novelty yarn, TDF, which stands for To Die For! The fun is in making this wild yarn, called a "mega boucle" into warp. Add the knitting accent or you'll weave a little wider in the version for non-knitters.*
>
> ## *Degree of Difficulty: Intermediate*

Details on this challenge: The key to turning this mega boucle into warp is isolating it in the slots while you alternate with a more regular yarn in the holes.

12 epi, 12 ppi for body, 5 epi, 5-6 ppi for collar. Knitting gauge = 21 stitches over 4" in pattern.

Sizes	Regular	Large-XL	Plus	
Bust Size	32"-38"	40"-46"	48"-54"	**See p. 102 for finished measurements.**
Yards used for A1	608 (670)	709 (781)	761 (825)	**Yardage in parenthesis at left is for non-knit.**
Yards used for A2	723 (700)	852 (825)	910 (878)	
Yards used for B	60 (68)	72 (80)	75 (84)	
Yards used for C	27	28	28	
Yards used for D	28	30	30	

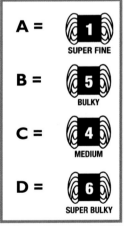

A = **1** SUPER FINE

B = **5** BULKY

C = **4** MEDIUM

D = **6** SUPER BULKY

Equipment
Loom with minimum 15 (18)" weaving width for knitter's version or 18 (20)" for non-knitters
12 and 5 dent reeds
2 shuttles
US 2, 32" circular needle
Crochet hook to pick up stitches (a no handle hook works best)
Steam iron, sewing machine, thread, and pins

Materials
A 1= 3 (4, 4) balls for knit version, 4 (4, 4) for non-knit, Mango Moon Mulberry Meadow, 75% superwash merino wool, 25% silk in Brook, 50 gm = 218 yards.

A2 = 4 (4, 5) balls, both versions, Mango Moon Mulberry Meadow in Reflection, 50 gm = 218 yards.

B = 1 skein for knitters option, 1 (2, 2) for non-knitters, Mango Moon Silk Ribbon, 45% silk, 38% viscose, 17% nylon in Juno. 75 yard skein.

C = 1 skein Berroco Maya, 85% cotton, 15% alpaca in 5638 Mancora, 1.75 ox = 136 yards.

D = 1 skein Mango Moon TDF, 75% Merino Wool, 18% Silk, 7% Nylon in Jupiter, 100 gm = 33 yds.

1/2 (1-1/2, 1-3/4) yards double fold, bias seam binding.

Yarn Advice

When you weave the collar, you will not get a straight fell line due to the slubs and inclusions of the TDF. Just let the weft meander gently across. See a close up of the fabric on p. 32. You can use a fork, tapestry beater or hair pick to assist in beating the weft where it sticks if desired.

Warp Body Pieces (with 12 dent reed) using A1 and B according to the chart and size you are choosing below. Size changes are in parenthesis.

Knitters:

14-3/4 (16-1/2, 16-1/2)" wide
178 (198, 198) ends
134 (142, 150)" long

	8 (9, 9) x		
18		18	A1
	2		B

Non-Knitters:

16-1/2 (18-1/4, 18-1/4)" wide
198 (218, 218) ends
134 (142), 150" long

	9 (10,10)x		
18		18	A1
	2		B

Weave Body Pieces (make 3) with A2 in plain weave, make 2 pieces for fronts, 25 (27, 29)" long each and 1 piece for the back, 60 (64, 68)" long. Weave 2 picks of scrap yarn between each piece to separate.

Weave a 1/2" footer with scrap yarn when all pieces are complete which is just like a header, but at the end. This will protect the end from unraveling before machine finishing.

Finish Cut the work from the loom. Double zigzag stitch along the beginning and ending edges of each piece before cutting the pieces apart and trimming away the scrap yarn (see p. 15, raw finish). Wash with the collar piece when complete.

Warp Collar (with 5 dent reed) 6" wide. There will be 29 ends at 69 (72, 72)" long per the charts below. These represent the heddle with grey shaded areas as slots and white areas with 0 as your heddles. #1 shows where your yarn will go as you draw the loops, then #2 shows how it looks once you turn the front of the loom toward you and sley the reed.

To describe the steps: as you draw loops, *pull 1 loop of D through a slot, one loop of C through the adjacent hole, then skip 1 slot and 1 hole. Repeat from * a total of 7 times. After the last skipped hole and slot, draw 1 loop of D through the slot. Cut and tie D at the warping peg so that the last slot has just 1 strand in it. Wind on and turn the loom to sley the reed from the front. Starting at the right, leave the single strand of D where it is, pull 1 of the double strands of C in the hole to the empty hole to its right. Pull 1 of the double strands of D to the empty slot to its right. Repeat across, filling all empty slots and holes.

Tie on as usual.

Warp Order:

1. **Draw Loops**

Facing back of loom.

Each stroke is a loop (2 strands) except final D (single strand).

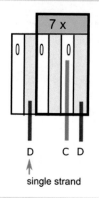

D C D

↑ single strand

2. **Sley Reed**

Front of loom.

Each stroke is a single strand.

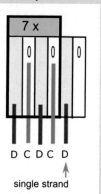

D C D C D

↑ single strand

Weave Collar with A2 in plain weave until piece measures 45 (48, 48)" under tension. This piece will turn out slightly longer than necessary to ensure that it does not come up short when fitting around the neckline. Your finished piece, before trimming, will be approximately 5-1/2" wide x 40-1/2 (43, 43)" long.

Finish

Weave a 1/2" footer when completed and cut from the loom. Raw finish both ends with a double zigzag.

Hand wash all pieces in room temperature water with mild detergent. Handle the collar piece gently and do not agitate. Hang dry and trim hanging tails flush. Cut 1 piece of seam binding 46 (55, 63)" long, wash, and dry.

Assemble

If choosing the knitted trim, add this first to the front pieces according to the instructions on the opposite page.

For both options, sew the underarm seam by matching the sleeve front pieces to the outer edges of the back panel, right sides together. Sew from the outer edge inward 17-1/2" on each side using a skinny seam (2 warp ends as seam allowance).

For non-knitters option, with right sides of fronts and back still together, sew the shoulder seams at each side using a skinny seam along the full length of the sleeves.

For knitted trim, place the right side of the knitted edge of each front piece onto the right side of the back panels 1/2" inward from the sleeve opening edge (the raw finish edges of the front and back woven parts will overhang the knitting by 1/2" for hemming later). On the woven side, sew along the full length of the knitting to attach to the back panel with a skinny seam.

Hem sleeves, both options: turn the woven fabric 1/2" to the wrong side at each sleeve opening end and press. Sew close to the raw finish edge.

Insert collar: starting at one side of the front opening, overlap the collar piece 1/2" onto the right side of the raw finish edge of this front piece. Pin it to overlap this side, around the back edge of the back panel, and back down over the raw finish edge of the other front piece. Pin carefully and sew around the collar close to the edge. Sew around again, 1/4" away. If the collar overhangs too much at one side, double zig zag and trim it to match.

Attach seam binding around the bottom edge. To trim the bottom opening all the way around, follow the instructions on p. 84 for finishing the neck opening of the sport top. You will attach a single piece of binding easing it around the underarm seams. Your shrug is ready to wear either open or with a shawl pin at the front.

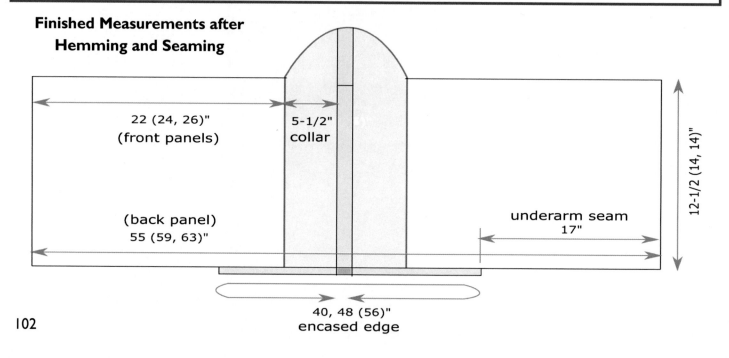

Finished Measurements after Hemming and Seaming

22 (24, 26)" (front panels)

5-1/2" collar

(back panel) 55 (59, 63)"

underarm seam 17"

12-1/2 (14, 14)"

40, 48 (56)" encased edge

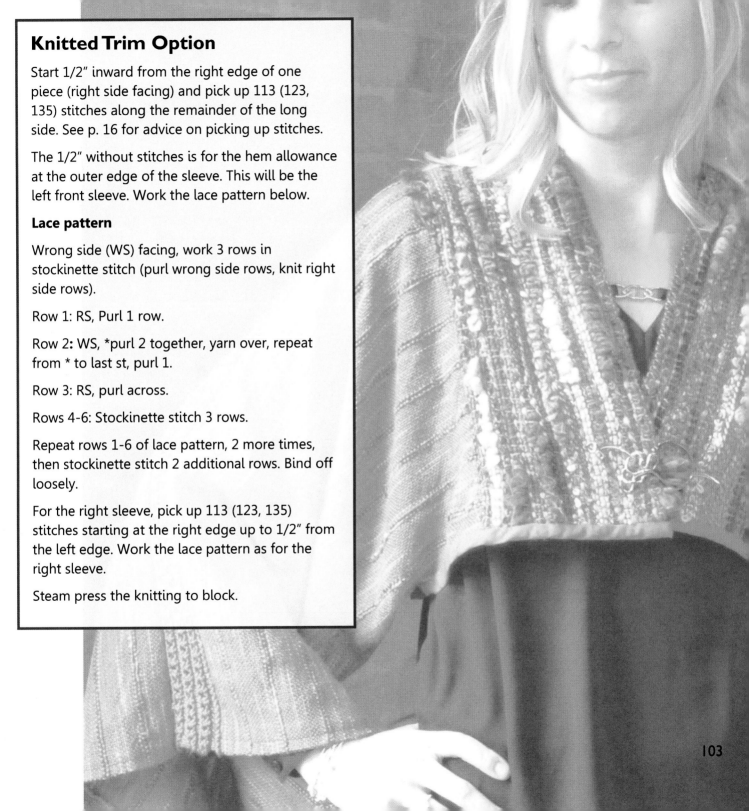

Knitted Trim Option

Start 1/2" inward from the right edge of one piece (right side facing) and pick up 113 (123, 135) stitches along the remainder of the long side. See p. 16 for advice on picking up stitches.

The 1/2" without stitches is for the hem allowance at the outer edge of the sleeve. This will be the left front sleeve. Work the lace pattern below.

Lace pattern

Wrong side (WS) facing, work 3 rows in stockinette stitch (purl wrong side rows, knit right side rows).

Row 1: RS, Purl 1 row.

Row 2: WS, *purl 2 together, yarn over, repeat from * to last st, purl 1.

Row 3: RS, purl across.

Rows 4-6: Stockinette stitch 3 rows.

Repeat rows 1-6 of lace pattern, 2 more times, then stockinette stitch 2 additional rows. Bind off loosely.

For the right sleeve, pick up 113 (123, 135) stitches starting at the right edge up to 1/2" from the left edge. Work the lace pattern as for the right sleeve.

Steam press the knitting to block.

103

FIND
YOUR
UNIQUE
TEXTURE!

Hikoo Caribou is a knitting novelty that is primarily used for making teddy bears. I just couldn't resist finding a home for it in this snugly swoncho (part sweatshirt, part poncho). Knitted cuffs bring the front and back together. The swoncho can be made without the cuffs for non-knitters.

Degree of Difficulty: Intermediate

Details on this challenge: Once again our rigid heddle shines in handling hairy, fuzzy, lumpy, fabulous yarns. You'll have a tough time discerning this fabric from knitting except that is works up much faster!

8 epi, 9 ppi for shoulder insets, 5 epi, 7 ppi for body

Approximate finished dimensions are diagramed on p. 108. One Size Fits Most

Equipment

Loom with minimum 15" weaving width

5 and 8 dent reeds

1 shuttle

Steam iron, sewing machine, thread, and pins

24" OR 32" circular needles or a set of double points in US 8 for knitting the cuffs in the round

Stitch marker

11 –12 warp sticks to weave between the pieces to reserve fringe

Materials

A = 5 balls Stacy Charles Astrakan, 55% Merino Wool, 28% Polyamide, 10% Alpaca, 7% Acrylic in color 4926, 50 gm = 87 yards (uses 392 yards).

B = 2 balls Hikoo Caribou, 100% Nylon in 002 black, 50 gm = 93 yards (uses 125 yards).

C = 2 skeins Berroco Ultra Alpaca, 50% superfine alpaca, 50% Peruvian wool, in Charcoal Mix, 100 gm = 219 yards (uses 395 yards).

D = 2 balls Schoppel Wolle Reggae Ombre, 100% merino in color 2306, 50 gm = 110 yards (uses 148 yards).

1 yard double fold, bias seam binding.

Yarn Advice

You won't see a lot of definition between warp and weft when you weave the front and back body pieces, so don't worry too much about your ppi here.

The shoulder insets are woven with a yarn (D) that transitions in color as you weave. I wasn't concerned about making those transitions symmetrical between the 2 pieces.

If you prefer symmetry, find a point on the first ball of D right where the color begins to change. Then take the second ball of D and try to locate the same point in that ball. Holding the strands together, pull yarn away from the balls and watch to see if they transition the same. You may have to wind off a fair amount as the color runs are long. If they appear to match as the color changes, great. If not, you can pull on the strands here to help them match, then back up to their beginning, and cut them for similar starting points. Fully load a different shuttle for each ball, starting and ending at the same color point. This may not be exact but should be close. You will weave each piece with a different shuttle.

For non-Knitters, do without the sleeves to create a poncho effect. Rather than machine finishing and cutting away the outside fringe from all edges of the shoulder insets, use the extra warp ends from the loom waste at the beginning and end of the weaving to tie fringe tassels at one end of each of the inset pieces and raw finishing and hemming the other end of each piece. Once assembled, tacking the front and back together just under each inset at the fringe ends will give you a sleeve opening and hold the poncho together.

Warp Body Pieces (5 dent reed) 14-3/4" wide x 125" long alternating loops of A then B, 18 times and end with A. (74 ends).

Weave Body Pieces (make 2) with A in plain weave for 45", Weave warp sticks between this and the next piece to reserve 11" for fringe. Weave the 2nd piece for 45".

Remove from the loom tying fringe tassels on both ends. Cut the warp reserved for fringe between the pieces, leaving approximately 5-1/2" fringe each side, remove the warp sticks, and tie fringe tassels on these ends also.

Warp Shoulder Insets (8 dent reed) 14-3/4" wide (118 ends) x 64" long with C.

Weave Shoulder Insets (make 2) with D in plain weave for 20". Weave 2 picks of scrap yarn, then plain weave the 2nd piece for 20" (using the second shuttle prepared as above if symmetry is desired). Weave a 1/2" scrap footer at the end to protect the ending edge. Raw finish each end, (p. 15). If you are not knitting cuffs, tie fringe on one end of each piece.

Finish

Hand wash all pieces in room temperature water with mild detergent. Hang dry and trim hanging tails flush. Cut 2 pieces of seam binding 15" long, wash, and dry.

Assemble

Finish one end of each shoulder inset with seam binding to create a "folded hem with wide encased edge" as instructed at the top of p. 96.

To set up the other end for sleeves, fold 1/2" to the wrong side and press. Sew this hem close to the raw finish edge. I call this a "raw finish hem". You will pick up knit stitches along this folded edge, after assembly, per instructions on the opposite page.

Create overlap seams to attach shoulder insets to body pieces. At the left edge of a body piece (right side facing up) overlap the long edge of an inset piece (also right side up) by 1/2". The raw finish hem just sewn will line up with the left end of the body piece. The encased edge of the inset will be towards the center. Pin carefully and sew close to the selvage of the body piece through all thicknesses. Sew again 1/4" away. Repeat to attach the other inset on the right side of this body piece.

For the back side, overlap the 2nd body piece 1/2" on the other long edge of the shoulder insets and sew close to the selvage, then 1/4" away.

Finished measurements after Assembly

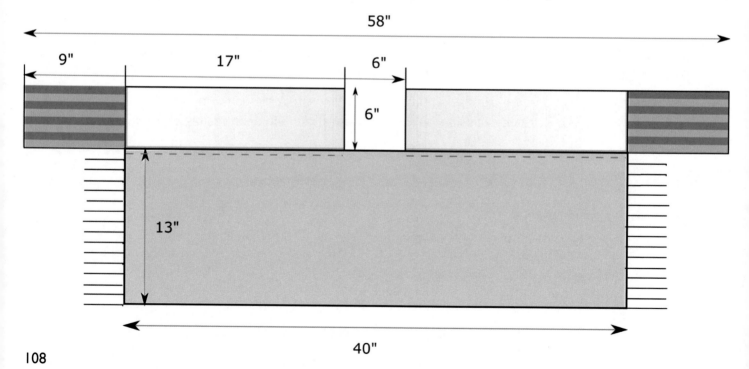

Knitted Sleeves

With a crochet hook, pick up 56 stitches along the outer hemmed edge of a shoulder inset and place them on knitting needles. See p. 16 for advice on this.

Join to work in the round. I like to use circular needles with the magic loop technique. There are many good videos on the internet to demonstrate magic loop if you are not already familiar. You may prefer to divide the stitches among double pointed needles instead.

Place marker for beginning of the round and work in knit 2, purl 2 around for 9". Bind off loosely. Repeat for the other sleeve.

The crochet finish around the neckline as seen in the model is optional and is simply 2 rows of single crochet at each side of the neck opening using C. The width of the opening has been reduced in the pattern to eliminate the crochet requirement.

BRING COLOR AND TEXTURE TOGETHER!

Waffle weave is not just for towels! The weave used to trim this piece alternates warp and weft floats to create a sculptural depth that is a great contrast to plain weave. Here, I use a version of waffle weave that doubles the pick-up rows for a dynamic accent to the sleeves and collar of this colorful poncho.

Degree of Difficulty: Intermediate

Details on this challenge: To show off the color range of our gradient yarn, we'll interweave with black for intensity and contrast and a bright red solid to reinforce the color notes. Gradient yarns (slow color transitions) make awesome weft that is full of surprises as you weave. You won't appreciate the full effect of the color transitions until your weaving comes off the loom.

8 epi, 9 ppi for plain weave of body, 10 epi, 17-18 ppi for waffle weave pattern of sleeve trim, 12 epi, 18-19 ppi for waffle weave pattern of collar

Approximate Finished Dimensions are diagramed on p. 116.
One Size Fits Most

Equipment

Loom with minimum 24" weaving width

8, 10 and 12 dent reeds

2 shuttles

1 pick-up stick to accommodate the 6-1/2" warp width of sleeve trim

Sewing machine, thread, and pins

Steam Iron

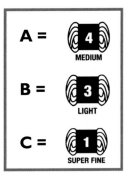

A = 4 MEDIUM

B = 3 LIGHT

C = 1 SUPER FINE

Materials

A = 3 balls Schoppel Gradient, 100% merino in color 2199, 100gm = 284 yards (uses 636 yards).

B1 = 3 skeins Hikoo Simplicity, 55% merino superwash, 18% acrylic, 17% nylon in Gypsy Red, 50gm = 117 yards, (uses 314 yards).

B2 = 5 skeins Hikoo Simplicity in Black, (uses 523 yards).

C = 4 skeins Hikoo CoBaSi, 55% cotton, 16% bamboo, 8% silk, 21% elastic nylon in Black, 50gm = 220 yards (uses 766 yds).

Yarn Advice

Sometimes when I am weaving larger pieces at a wide sett with soft yarns, I find that it can be a challenge to keep my fell line (the last pick woven) straight, despite best efforts at tensioning and weaving with consistency. If you have checked your tension and you have a few errant ends that need to be tightened, you can hang a weight from the thread at the back of the loom in the form of an S hook with a metal washer (see right). If that is not the issue, one assist is to pack warp sticks onto the front beam with the fabric as you roll it forward. This, and/or a single warp stick pushed into the back open shed, can sharpen things up nicely.

I thought that the elastic content in C would create problems as warp, like gathering or substantial shrinkage, but I found that the resulting fabric shrank less than anticipated (about 15-18% overall) and stayed flat with the textured weave. When using C on C for the collar, however, draw-in and shrinkage was nearly 30%. Elastic in the fiber can be tricky as you can see and should be tested before you design with it.

If you are sensitive to wool around your neck, the content of C, CoBaSi, is very "next to skin friendly".

Warp Body (8 dent reed)

24" wide x 132" long with B1 and B2 according to the warp order chart at right. See p. 12 for chart reading advice if needed. This chart gives you the number of inches, rather than ends, for simplicity. End count in unimportant here.

	10-1/2"		B1
8"		5-1/2"	B2

Weave Body (weave 2)

with A and B2 according to the weaving order chart at right for a total of 54". Measure carefully as you will make 2 matching pieces on this warp. When 1st one is complete. Weave 2 picks of scrap yarn and repeat the sequence for the 2nd piece. End with a 1/2" footer of scrap yarn to protect then ending edge until finishing, cut the work from the loom, and set the pieces aside,

A	B2
	7"
17"	
	6"
17"	
	7"

Warp Armhole Trim (10 dent reed)

6-3/4" wide x 124" long (68 ends) with C.

Weave Armhole Trim (weave 2)

In heddle down position, set your pick-up stick behind the reed picking up the first 2 warp ends on top of the stick, skipping over the next 2 from the top row only (these are slot threads). Repeat this across. End with 2 ends on top. Leave the stick pushed to the back beam throughout, out of the way until it is used on pick-up rows. Steps 2 and 4 are weft floats. Steps 7 and 9 are warp floats. It is assumed (not stated) that you will throw the shuttle through the shed made on each step of the pattern below.

Weave with A in the following pattern for 48". Weave 2 picks of scrap yarn, then weave a 2nd identical piece. Weave a 1/2" footer of scrap yarn at the end and cut the work from the loom.

1. Heddle up.
2. Pick-up stick (place reed in neutral, pull stick forward and upright against reed).
3. Heddle up.
4. Repeat step 2.
5. Heddle up.
6. Heddle down.
7. Heddle up and pick-up stick (place reed in up position, pull stick forward and leave flat against the reed).\
8. Heddle down.
9. Repeat step 7.
10. Heddle down.

Finish

Raw finish all ends of the body pieces before cutting them apart between the 2 scrap picks and trimming away all scrap (see p. 15). Raw finish with **3 rows** of zigzag at each end of the sleeve trim as this edge will be exposed along the bottom of the garment and needs to be more secure. Trim away all scrap.

Warp Collar (12 dent reed) 12-1/4" wide x 68" long (146 ends) with C. Set the pick-up stick as you did for the trim pieces.

Weave Collar in the 10 step waffle weave pattern until the piece measures 42". Remove from the loom tying 4 strand tassels on each end.

Finish by hand washing all pieces with mild detergent in room temperature water and hang dry. Trim fringe on the collar to 6".

Assemble Shoulder Seams

With the narrower stripe of black at the top, pin the 2 pieces together along the top edge, working to match the stripes on each piece. It is common for the pieces to be slightly off in length, so pin from each outer edge inward. Any difference can be accommodated in the neck opening. Sew from the outer edges in, leaving 13" open in the middle as shown in the drawing below. You'll use a skinny seam allowance (2 warp ends at selvage).

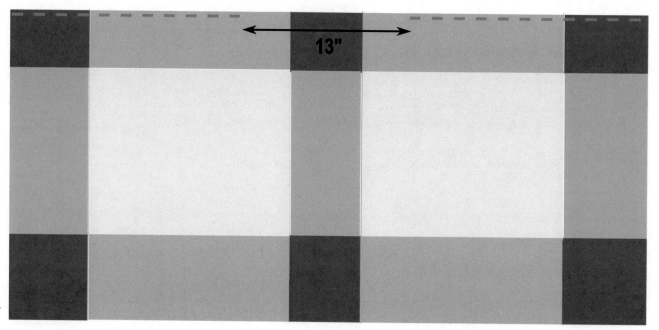

Attach Side Trim

Open the poncho out flat so the right sides are facing up. Starting at the left edge, place one trim piece along the raw finish edge of the poncho from the left selvage across to the right selvage (right sides together). You may find that the trim piece is slightly longer when you get to the right. This was planned to minimize the problem that this piece might come up short. The raw finish edges of the trim will need to line up with the bottom selvage of both the front and back when finished, so one side may need zigzagging again and trimming as you match it to the poncho.

Pin the trim to the poncho carefully. Now you can triple zigzag stitch and trim any excess at the end (if needed). Even it up before sewing the pieces together along the length with a 1/2" seam allowance. Turn the trim piece out and press the seam allowance in toward the center using a pressing cloth.

Attach Collar

Fold the collar piece in half so fringe ends meet. With the right side of the poncho out, place the collar inside the neck opening, with the fold at the right shoulder seam (see photo below). Fringe ends of collar will be off to the left. Pin and sew the collar in place around the neck. Starting at the left shoulder seam at the back, sew the pieces together all the way around the collar edge with 1/4" seam allowance. Be careful to avoid catching the loose fringed edges in your sewing.

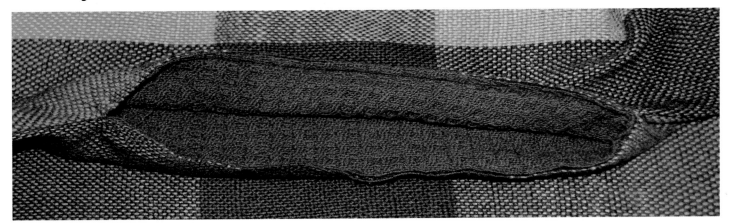

Turn the collar out. The neckline seam will show on the outside. The collar will hang downward to conceal this when wearing.

Sew Underarm Seams

Prepare to sew, with the right sides out, along the inner edge of the black stripes of the body for underarm seams. Pin through both thicknesses to try to line up the black stripe edges between the front and back pieces. Sew along the black stripes from bottom upward to 11" as shown in the diagram below.

Finished Measurements after Seaming and Trim

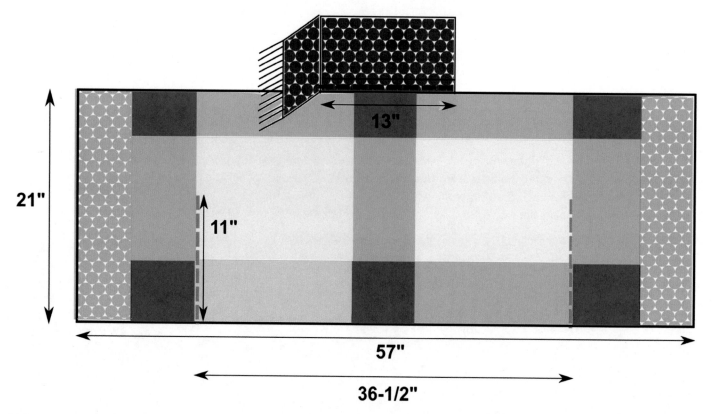

Resources

BOOKS and VIDEOS by TAMARA POFF

Woven Style for the 15" Rigid Heddle Loom, Dec. 2016

Available at
amazon

New! Video courses at

weavingwithpoffstudio.com

Rigid Heddle Weaving: Learn to Weave with the V Cowl

This is a course to teach the basics from A-Z to the new weaver, along with extensive advice on how to improve technique. Students will complete the very popular V cowl.

Weaving the V Cowl on the Rigid Heddle Loom

This one is pattern oriented for weavers who can warp on their own. You'll also get additional advice regarding yarn choices and weaving tips to improve your work.

Sign up for new course, book, and pattern announcements at www.poffstudio.com and find help on YouTube at Poffstudio.

YARN COMPANIES and SUPPLIERS

Many thanks to the following companies for their support.

Berroco, berroco.com
401-769-1212

Hamilton Yarns
hamiltonyarns.com

Interlacements Yarns, interlacementsyarns.com
920-826-5970

Malabrigo, malabrigoyarn.com
US 786-427-1048

Mango Moon Yarns, Be Sweet, and Vinni's Colors
Recently retired. Their yarns can be obtained from
Humble Acres Yarn, humbleacresyarn.com
517-455-7160

Mary Gavan Yarns
marygavanyarns.com

Misti Alpaca, mistialpaca.com
888-776-9276

Prism Yarn
prismyarn.com

Skacel, skacelknitting.com
425-291-9600

Tahki Stacy Charles, tahkistacycharles.com
718-326-4433

Winderfull
thewinderfull.com
561-495-1095

About the Author

Tamara (Tammy) Poff is on a mission to help fiber enthusiasts expand their creative range with just simple tools. With patterns, books, online courses as well as free downloads and YouTube videos, she seeks to reach out to rigid heddle weavers to make the craft ever more accessible. She'll take you "beyond the rectangle" with both traditional and nontraditional ideas.

A painter, a weaver, a knitter, and a recent transplant to Tucson, Arizona, Tammy is lovin' the life of the mountains in between traveling and teaching weaving throughout the US.

Find more or contact her at www.poffstudio.com.

Made in United States
Orlando, FL
22 September 2024

51804471R00066